Beethoven's Lives

Beethoven's Lives

The Biographical Tradition

Lewis Lockwood

THE BOYDELL PRESS

First published 2020
The Boydell Press, Woodbridge

ISBN 978–1-78327–551–9

The Boydell Press is an imprint of Boydell & Brewer Ltd
PO Box 9, Woodbridge, Suffolk IP12 3DF, UK
and of Boydell & Brewer Inc.
668 Mt Hope Avenue, Rochester, NY 14620–2731, USA
website: www.boydellandbrewer.com

The publisher has no responsibility for the continued existence or
accuracy of URLs for external or third-party internet websites referred
to in this book, and does not guarantee that any content on such
websites is, or will remain, accurate or appropriate

A catalogue record of this publication is available
from the British Library

This publication is printed on acid-free paper

Printed and bound in Great Britain by TJ International Ltd, Padstow, Cornwall

Contents

List of Illustrations	vii
Preface	ix
Acknowledgments	xix
List of Abbreviations	xxi

1. The Earliest Biographers — 1

Grillparzer's Funeral Oration, 1827 — 1

Contemporary Observers — 3

Early Attempts and Rivalries — 5

Wegeler and Ries, 1838 — 9

2. Beethoven Biography, 1840–*c.* 1875 — 15

The Emergence of Beethoven Biography — 15

Anton Schindler as Biographer and Falsifier, 1840–60 — 18

Alexander Wheelock Thayer and the Pursuit of Truth:
His Earlier Work, 1849–66 — 31

Lenz, Marx, and Nohl — 41

Nottebohm on the Composer at Work — 47

Richard Wagner and G. E. Anders: A Projected
Beethoven Biography (1841) — 51

3. The Late Nineteenth and Early Twentieth Centuries — 65

The Newly Enlarged Context for Beethoven Biography — 65

Beethoven Biographies and Related Works, *c.* 1870–1927 — 68

Thayer's Later Contributions, 1867–97 — 69

German Biographers, *c.* 1870–1935 — 75

The French Tradition: Romain Rolland; Vincent D'Indy;
    others   85

The English Tradition: George Grove; Donald Francis
    Tovey; Marion Scott; J. W. N. Sullivan   90

4. **Beethoven Biography and European Politics, 1933–77**   103

German Beethoven Scholarship in the Nazi Period
    (1933–45)   103

East Germany and West Germany, 1945–77   108

Austrian Beethoven Conferences, 1970 and 1977   110

Bonn, Berlin, and Detroit, 1970 and 1977   112

5. **The Modern Era**   117

The Bicentenary Year 1970: Two Contrasting Biographies   117

Maynard Solomon, 1977 and 1998   119

Kerman, Tyson, and Kropfinger, 1980 and 2000   123

Recent Biographies   129

Other Recent Biographies   137

6. **Exploring Beethoven's Life and Work:**
    Three Sample Years   145

1787: The Young Beethoven's Journey to Vienna   146

1809: War; the Archduke Rudolph   154

1826: The Final Phase; the Late Quartets; Karl's
    Attempted Suicide; the Last Months   162

7. **Reminiscences and Reflections**   169

Future Prospects   178

Bibliography   183
Index   199

Illustrations

Illustrations 1–8: pp. 57–64
Illustrations 9–13: pp. 100–102
Illustrations 14–18: pp. 142–144
Illustrations 19–21: pp. 166–168

1. Karl Holz: photograph of a miniature portrait by Betty Frölich. Beethoven-Haus Bonn, NE 81, Band I, No. 1107. Used by permission.

2. Ferdinand Ries portrait: anonymous oil painting. Beethoven-Haus Bonn, B 210. Used by permission.

3. Franz Wegeler portrait: painting by Johann Heinrich Richter. Beethoven-Haus Bonn, B 2050. Used by permission.

4. Anton Schindler: reproduction of a photograph. Beethoven-Haus Bonn, B 1393; K 43/17. Used by permission.

5. Alexander Wheelock Thayer: photograph by Emil Koch (1890). Beethoven-Haus Bonn, B 1371. Used by permission.

6. Ludwig Nohl, *Der Lehrkörper Ruperto Carola zu Heidelberg im Jahre 500 ihres Bestehen* (Heidelberg, 1886).

7. Gustav Nottebohm, by permission of Brahms-Institut an der Musikhochschule Lübeck.

8. Theodor Frimmel (1853–1928), photograph by Alois Beer. Beethoven-Haus Bonn, B 1299. Used by permission.

9. Paul Bekker © Max Nehrdich, Kassel.

10. Romain Rolland, Agence de presse Meurisse, by permission of Bibliothèque nationale de France.

11. Sir George Grove, Elliot and Fry © National Portrait Gallery, London.

12. Sir Donald Francis Tovey, William Rothenstein © National Portrait Gallery, London.

13. J. W. N. Sullivan, Lady Ottoline Morrel © National Portrait Gallery, London.

14. Maynard Solomon, private collection, by kind permission of Eva Solomon.

15. Joseph Kerman © Kathleen Karn.

16. Alan Tyson © The British Academy.

17. William Kinderman © Anna Kinderman.

18. Barry Cooper, private collection.

19. Beethoven as a Youth: Lithograph by the Becker Brothers of a Joseph Neesen silhouette of Ludwig van Beethoven, age 15. Beethoven-Haus Bonn, 91.211. Used by permission.

20. Beethoven in Middle Age: Drawing by Ludwig Ferdinand Schnorr von Carolsfeld, 1810. Beethoven-Haus Bonn, B 2380, K 67/Unger-Mappe 8. Used by permission.

21. Beethoven in Old Age: Lithograph from a drawing by Johann Stephan Decker, 1824. Beethoven-Haus Bonn, B 285. Used by permission.

The author and publisher are grateful to all the institutions and individuals listed for permission to reproduce the materials in which they hold copyright. Every effort has been made to trace the copyright holders; apologies are offered for any omission, and the publisher will be pleased to add any necessary acknowledgement in subsequent editions.

Preface

THE BEETHOVEN SCULPTURE ON the cover of this book was made around 1907 by Max Klinger. It is a smaller version of the monumental figure that Klinger had created for the Vienna Secession House Exhibit in 1902, in which Beethoven sits enthroned, with polychrome drapery upon his knees. This less elaborate sculpture, showing only Beethoven's torso, had been ordered by the Viennese art patron Karl Wittgenstein for his music room. Subsequently it passed to his son, the pianist Paul Wittgenstein, who gave it to the Boston Museum of Fine Arts in 1962.[1]

In both versions Klinger portrays Beethoven the man, naked before the world, resolute, fists clenched, peering into the distance. If we move from the domain of imagery to that of biography, I would suggest that all the writers whom I will discuss in the following chapters, including myself, are seeking to find ways to clothe the figure imaginatively, to bring the artist and the man to life, and to enable the reader to try to reach beyond the basic experience of Beethoven's music to the man himself. The search is for Beethoven, as best we can determine, as he was in his age and in his lifetime – with the understanding that each biographer sees him according to his own perspectives, his own background, and his own cultural framework.

This book offers a critical and comparative review of Beethoven biography. It begins with the first attempts in the early nineteenth century, then moves through the longer

---

[1] I am grateful to the Boston MFA for permission to reproduce this image. For a discussion of the original sculpture see Alessandra Comini, *The Changing Image of Beethoven: A Study in Mythmaking* (New York: Rizzoli, 1987), 388–415.

history of the genre and comes down into our own time. Over nearly two hundred years since Beethoven's death in 1827, many book-length interpretations of his life and work have appeared, mainly in German, French, and English, though also of course in other languages. Years ago I compared Beethoven biographers to portrait painters:

> For no matter how faithfully painters work to present their subjects, they also present themselves. Each has an individual point of view, a vision of the subject that determines what the essential proportions, colors, and textures will be, what features will be thrust into the foreground and what will remain in the background or be omitted altogether.[2]

As a personal note, I have been teaching and writing in the field of Beethoven scholarship since the 1960s, and much of my work has centered on the study of the primary musical sources of his works – mainly Beethoven's sketches and autograph manuscripts, the documents that give us insight into his inner world as a composer. In 2003, at the invitation of my friend Michael Ochs, then Music Editor at W. W. Norton, I ventured into Beethoven biography with my own book, *Beethoven: The Music and the Life.* In that book I tried to come to grips with the larger picture of his life and works, but with an admitted bias towards the music. A few years later, in 2007, I was invited by David M. Hertz of Indiana University to take part in a symposium on Beethoven biography, and, as I note in the Acknowledgments the result was an essay that became the precursor of the present volume.[3]

The bulk of this book is made up of brief portrayals of Beethoven biographers, their work and their contexts. In the nineteenth-century sections experienced readers will

---

[2] Lewis Lockwood, *Beethoven: The Music and the Life,* (New York: Norton, 2003), xviii.

[3] Lewis Lockwood, "Reappraising Beethoven Biography," *Yearbook of General and Comparative Literature* 53 (2007), 83–99.

find familiar names, those of Anton Schindler and Alexander Wheelock Thayer. They may be surprised to find Gustav Nottebohm, the pioneering scholar of the Beethoven sketchbooks, but, as I will show, there is good reason to believe that Nottebohm saw his intensive study of the composer's formation of his works at early stages as a type of biography. They will be even more surprised to find among the biographers, or would-be biographers, none other than the young Richard Wagner. I include Wagner not by virtue of his famous critical essays on Beethoven and his lifetime reverence for him, but also because, in his early days in Paris, around 1841, Wagner actually thought of collaborating on a carefully researched biography of Beethoven, which did not happen.

Besides my critical survey of Beethoven biographers, I provide three chapters as sample discussions of the abiding problem of how we can understand and attempt to portray the modes of relationship between the artist's life and his work. These sections will focus on these specific years – 1787, 1809, and 1826. The year 1787 shows Beethoven at sixteen as a gifted young musician at Bonn, a brilliant pianist and composer, hailed by his patrons as a second Mozart. It is the year of his first trip to Vienna, almost certainly in the hope of meeting Mozart, a journey about which we have learned some important new facts in the past ten years. The year 1809 sees Beethoven in the fullness of his artistic maturity, with the Fifth and Sixth symphonies and the Opus 59 Quartets behind him. It is the year of the 'Lebewohl' piano sonata, a deeply felt reflection on the departure from Vienna of his most important patron, the Archduke Rudolph. It is also the year of other major works, including the completion of the 'Emperor' Concerto, Opus 73, the string quartet Opus 74, the Fantasy for piano Opus 77, and two other piano sonatas Opus 78 and Opus 79. All this takes place in 1809 against the background of the bombardment and invasion of Vienna by the Napoleonic armies, about which Beethoven comments in letters. My final sample chapter is on 1826, the last full year of Beethoven's life, in which he composed his last string quartets, Opus 131 and Opus 135. We see him working now at the summit of his artistic powers, despite his illnesses, his physical debilitation, his sometimes aberrant behavior, and the pain and grief brought on by his nephew Karl's attempted suicide in August of that year.

In the final chapter, I comment on my own work and on Beethoven biography in its relationship to the wider domain of artistic biography. In doing so I am consciously drawing upon music history but also comparable works in literature and art, in which we find not only lives of famous figures but also a few attempts to survey the biographical traditions that surround them. One is the arresting study by Samuel Schoenbaum of Shakespeare biographies entitled *Shakespeare's Lives*, from which I have learned a great deal and have shamelessly borrowed my title. Another is the book by my former Princeton colleague in art history, the late A. Richard Turner, whose book, *Inventing Leonardo*, is a critical overview of the interpretations of Leonardo da Vinci, as daunting a subject as can be imagined. Of course the surviving documents of the lives of Shakespeare and Leonardo are vastly different in scope, content, and significance, and they are unlike the evidence that survives for Beethoven. For Shakespeare we have scanty personal documentation beyond the plays and poems themselves. For Leonardo we have his paintings and other art-works, but also the famous notebooks that record his vast range of human and scientific interests. They form a partial and approximate parallel to the Beethoven sketchbooks, but range far more widely into other domains. As Martin Kemp has noted, Leonardo created in his notebooks a "great intellectual and visual edifice."[4] Beethoven's regular use of sketchbooks to shape and

---

[4] Martin Kemp, *Leonardo* (Oxford: Oxford University Press, 2004), 47.

work out the main lines and details of his works, from early in his career to the very end, was a deeply entrenched and regular practice that apparently gave his creative work a degree of regularity that contrasts sharply with the disorder of his outer life.

For Beethoven we have more than two thousand letters and related documents. Many of these have been known since the mid-19th century, but despite numerous earlier efforts to collect and publish them, the first truly reliable publication of their original texts in German came out in 1996, under the general editorship of Sieghard Brandenburg.[5] And yet, important correspondence can still come to light, as with the recent discovery of a letter that Beethoven wrote in 1795, soon after his arrival in Vienna. Writing to Heinrich von Struve, a friend from Bonn now in Russia, he comments on the fact that in the Russia of his time men are treated beneath their dignity, and he wonders "when the time will come in which there will be only people [*Menschen*] in the world." By "Menschen" Beethoven clearly means humanity as a whole, not princes, counts, or barons, divided from the common people by social class. This letter, discovered in 2012 and published in 2018 by Julia Ronge, reflects Beethoven's awareness of the democratic ideals that had animated and informed the American and French revolutions, both of which had taken place during his youth.[6] It is a parallel to the lines in Schiller's "Ode to Joy" in which the poet proclaims that "All men shall become brothers" and then declares, "Oh you millions, I embrace you!" This is the poem that Beethoven knew in his youth, thought of setting

---

5 *Briefwechsel.*

6 See the publication, *"wann wird auch der Zeitpunkt kommen wo es nur Menschen geben wird," Ein unbekannter Brief Beethovens an Heinrich von Struve,* with commentary by Julia Ronge and facsimile, *Jahresgabe des Vereins Beethoven-Haus 2018* (Bonn: Beethoven-Haus, 2018), Heft 34.

to music for many years, and finally did, indelibly, in the Ninth Symphony.

Other important Beethoven documents on which biographers can draw include Beethoven's *Tagebuch*, or personal diary, of 1812–18, which was published by Maynard Solomon.[7] And from Beethoven's last years, 1818–27, we possess the many fascinating conversation books in which visitors wrote down comments and questions to the deaf composer and received his verbal replies. The conversation books have been fully available in German since 2001, edited by Karl-Heinz Köhler with Dagmar Beck and Grita Herre, and now the first complete and newly annotated English translations, by Theodore Albrecht, have begun to appear.[8] Of course, biographers at different periods have had varying degrees of access to these materials, but the most dedicated writers worked with what parts of them they had.

Perhaps even more than with other men of genius of past centuries, including Shakespeare and Leonardo, the image of Beethoven the man has become a cultural token in the

[7]   Edited by Maynard Solomon and published in these volumes:
      1) *Beethoven Studies 3*, ed. Alan Tyson (Cambridge: Cambridge University Press, 1982), 193–288; 2) A revised version in Maynard Solomon, *Beethoven Essays* (Cambridge, MA: Harvard University Press, 1988), 233–95; 3) Ludwig van Beethoven, *Beethovens Tagebuch*. Edited by Maynard Solomon and Sieghard Brandenburg. (Mainz: v. Hase & Koehler, 1990).
[8]   *Ludwig van Beethoven, Konversationshefte*, edited by Karl-Heinz Köhler with Dagmar Beck and Grita Herre, 11 volumes (Leipzig: VEB Deutscher Verlag, 1972–2001). The first three volumes of the projected complete English translation of the conversation books, edited and translated by Theodore Albrecht (Woodbridge: The Boydell Press) have appeared in 2018 (Vol. 1), 2019 (Vol. 2) and 2020 (Vol. 3); hereafter abbreviated as AlbrechtBC. My review of volumes 1 and 2, covering the material from February 1818 to September 1820, appeared in *The New York Review of Books*, Vol. LXVII, No. 5 (March 26, 2020), 51–2.

media-driven world of entertainment in which we now live. He is easily recognized by virtue of his flowing hair, broad features, and resolute expression, and he stands as perhaps the most visible figure in the world of classical music as it attempts to survive the transformations that have brought us the music industry in all its forms. But the true historical world in which Beethoven lived and composed, early to late – in genres ranging from his symphonies, his string quartets, his piano music, the opera *Fidelio*, and the choral works, all the way to his art songs, settings of folk songs and other works of all kinds – remains the subject of unceasing study by his devotees, not only in Europe and America but wherever his music is known and valued. Not to mention his lifetime struggles with deafness, isolation, loneliness, financial troubles, and interpersonal difficulties of all kinds.

Because this book is essentially confined to discussion of books dealing with Beethoven's life, with a few excursions, I need to say a few words about the status of biography in current serious writing about music across the main fields that are now prevalent in professional circles in musicology. I construe that word in the broadest sense to include music history, theory, and criticism, and in the current age of oncoming globalization I should clarify that I am referring here to the study of Western music in all its richness and complexity over the centuries. Within that vast terrain my focus is specifically on biography, a field that currently has limited recognition in professional circles but is readily familiar to many lay readers, to whom it offers a portal to further understanding of music they care deeply about.

To cast my net as widely as possible, I felt the need to bring in for discussion a fair number of writers who are scarcely household names, but who nevertheless deserve mention. I also have to stress that this book does not pretend to deal with important recent commentaries on Beethoven that are outside the area of biography – among them the influential writings of Carl Dahlhaus and Theodor Adorno. In the case of Dahlhaus, his major book on Beethoven, *Ludwig van Beethoven: Approaches to his Music* (a 1991 English translation of his *Beethoven in seiner Zeit*, of 1987) reveals his deep skepticism about the value of biography as having any true significance for the interpretation of the composer's works. In a characteristic passage he writes:

> ...as a general rule, the only role for a confirmed historical fact is to serve as one more component in a biographical narrative that runs along beside the interpretation of the work without making any important intervention in it...[9]

At best, for Dahlhaus, whose critical acumen is everywhere apparent when he is dealing with issues of musical substance, it is only the minor works of Beethoven – or, presumably, any other major composer – for which any aspect of his biography might be in any way illuminating. In his chapter on "Life and Work" Dahlhaus consistently endeavors to separate the "aesthetic subject" in the interpretation of the works from the "biographical subject," a separation on which he dwells at length.[10] Yet even so, a careful reading of Dahlhaus's comments on individual books and articles, which he lists in the extensive bibliography, shows his ability quietly to recognize the qualities of some earlier books on Beethoven written from viewpoints very different from his own, even including some of the best-known and essentially factual biographies, such as that of Thayer.

As for Adorno, whose writings on Beethoven are primarily conceived as philosophical rather than historical or analytical, his work emerges in the best-known compilation, in English, as a "diary of his experiences of Beethoven's

---

[9] Carl Dahlhaus, *Ludwig van Beethoven: Approaches to His Music*, translated by Mary Whittall (Oxford: Clarendon Press, 1991), 1.

[10] *Ibid.*, 30–41.

music," in the words of his editor, Rolf Tiedemann.[11] Along with perceptive remarks on individual works and with many references to Hegelian and Marxist philosophy and to a wide range of cultural abstractions, there is no place in Adorno's writings on Beethoven that I have found that make any room for discussion of the actualities of the composer's career, personality, relationships close and distant – in other words, the authentic and specific conditions of his life from start to finish.

Because so much work in all fields of musicology and music theory is addressed not to the broad public but to specialists, the literature of music biography, which tends inevitably towards the public sphere, lies pretty much outside the boundaries of these fields of research. One might think that with the current rise of cultural studies as a field of studies, biographies of important composers might find a place – but here too the opposite appears to be the case. Taking its basic orientation from the social sciences and the increasing globalization of music studies, the field in general seems to be developing ways of thought that embrace issues far beyond the lives and careers of individual composers or the critical and analytical study of individual works. Accordingly, close biographical narratives seem to be currently unlikely to be a much-cultivated subject. Instead, social and political issues tend to dominate the current horizon of scholarly interest more than ever before and, in this context, biography seems at best a peripheral subject.[12] Years ago a dedicated music theorist, immersed in the analysis of a

[11] Theodor W. Adorno, *Beethoven: The Philosophy of Music*, ed. Rolf Tiedemann (Stanford: Stanford University Press, 1998), ix.

[12] For samplings of the varied points of view embraced by cultural studies in music, see Martin Clayton, Trevor Herbert, and Richard Middleton, eds., *The Cultural Study of Music: A Critical Introduction* (New York: Routledge, 2003) and many publications since then.

particular work, said to me, "What do I care who wrote it?" The question continues to resound in my memory, and it raises a multitude of questions about the nature, character, and significance of what we generally take to be the various modes of comprehension of music as an art-form. For many listeners, for readers, for people with an interest in deepening their understanding of their musical experience in concert halls, through recordings, or streaming through the digital universe, I would argue that the question of "who wrote" a work that is being heard is not only not a trivial fact but is a portal to a wider and stronger grasp of the music that is being experienced. Not the only portal, of course, but an important one.

The reception of Beethoven's music by audiences all over the world is the central aspect of his broad legacy to the world. There is also another kind of reception, namely the efforts by scholars, critics, biographers, and theorists to portray him to their readers, that is another dimension of the vast subject. A large-scale study of all these endeavors has yet to be undertaken (the present book deals specifically with the biographers, despite some crossing of boundaries here and there). But at least one valuable essay deserves mention here: it is Scott Burnham's essay "The Four Ages of Beethoven: critical reception and the canonic composer."[13] As we live through 2020, the two hundred and fiftieth anniversary of his birth in 1770, I hope this book may contribute to a better understanding of his importance as man and artist. I offer it as a critical overview of the changing ways in which biographers have sought to portray Beethoven's life and works to a broad public.

Brookline, Massachusetts

2019

---

[13] Glenn Stanley, ed., *The Cambridge Companion to Beethoven* (Cambridge: Cambridge University Press, 2000), 272–291.

Acknowledgments

IN THE COURSE OF writing this book I have been greatly aided by organizations and by individuals, whose help I want to acknowledge. First, I am indebted to the Boston Museum of Fine Arts, with whose permission I am reproducing the Beethoven sculpture by Max Klinger that is on the cover of this book. Similarly, I am indebted to the Beethoven-Haus in Bonn for permission to reproduce the images I have used for illustrations (specific credits are shown with the images). And I am especially grateful to the editors of the *Yearbook of Comparative and General Literature* for permission to make use of some of the material in an article that I published in their pages in 2007 (Volume 53, 53–99) entitled "Reappraising Beethoven Biography."

The early chapters were read by Theodore Albrecht, who gave me valuable suggestions in the light of his remarkable knowledge of Beethoven's life and milieu. So did Grant William Cook, whose work on Alexander Wheelock Thayer is of very high value and who helped me with comments and corrections in my discussion of Thayer's achievements. On matters of style and approach I profited greatly from a close reading of the entire manuscript by my wife, Ava Bry Penman, as well as from her patience while I was scanning the horizon of the world of Beethoven biography and putting my observations together. I am also grateful to Lucy Turner, Scott Burnham, and Jessie Ann Owens, all of whom offered helpful ideas on various parts of this book. Most of all, my warmest gratitude goes to Megan Ross, who helped with every phase of the writing and who compiled the bibliography and the index. When she had to turn to other important personal matters, I was fortunate enough to be able to obtain the services of Matthew Cron, who shepherded the manuscript through the final stages of preparation. And finally, I am indebted to Michael Middeke, Nick Bingham, Elizabeth Howard and Megan Milan of Boydell and Brewer for their fine editorial work.

Brookline, MA

Abbreviations

AlbrechtBC   Beethoven, Ludwig van. *Beethoven's Conversation Books*. Edited and translated by Theodore Albrecht. Woodbridge: The Boydell Press, Vol. 1 Nos. 1–8, February 1818 to March 1820 (2018); Vol. 2 Nos. 9 to 16 (March 1820 to September 1820) (2019); Vol. 3 Nos. 17 to 31 (May 1822 to May 1823) (2020).

Anderson   Beethoven, Ludwig van. *The Letters of Beethoven*. Translated and edited by Emily Anderson. 3 vols. London: Macmillan, 1961; Reprint, 1985.

BBS   *Bonner Beethoven-Studien.*

BF   *Beethoven Forum.*

Briefwechsel   Beethoven, Ludwig van. *Briefwechsel: Gesamtausgabe*. Edited by Sieghard Brandenburg. 7 vols. Munich: G. Henle Verlag, 1996–98.

JAMS   *Journal of the American Musicological Society.*

JTW   Douglas Johnson, Alan Tyson and Robert Winter. *The Beethoven Sketchbooks: History, Reconstruction, Inventory*. Berkeley: University of California Press, 1985.

LvBWV   Kurt Dorfmüller, Norbert Gertsch, and Julia Ronge (eds). *Ludwig van Beethoven: Thematisch-Bibliographisches Werkverzeichnis*. 2 vols. Munich: G. Henle Verlag, 2014.

N I   Nottebohm, Gustav. *Beethoveniana*. Leipzig: Reiter-Biedermann, 1872.

N II   Nottebohm, Gustav. *Zweite Beethoveniana: Nachgelassene Aufsätze*. Leipzig, 1887.

TD   Thayer, Alexander Wheelock. *Ludwig van Beethovens Leben*, ed. Hermann Deiters, 3 vols. Berlin: Weber, 1866–79.

TDR   Thayer, Alexander Wheelock. *Ludwig van Beethovens Leben*. Edited by Hugo Riemann from the revised edition of Hermann Deiters (1901), Leipzig: Breitkopf & Härtel, 1908–1917.

TF   Thayer, Alexander Wheelock. *Thayer's Life of Beethoven*. 2 vols. Revised and edited by Elliot Forbes. Princeton: Princeton University Press, 1964.

TK   Thayer, Alexander Wheelock, *The Life of Ludwig van Beethoven*, 3 vols. Edited, revised and amended from the original English manuscript and the German edition of Hermann Deiters and Hugo Riemann, concluded, and all the documents newly translated by Henry Edward Krehbiel. New York: G. Schirmer for The Beethoven Association, 1921.

1

The Earliest Biographers

Grillparzer's Funeral Oration, 1827

"WHEN I HEARD OF Beethoven's death it seemed to me as if a god had departed, and I shed bitter tears" – such were the words of the German-born conductor Charles Hallé, later the founder of the Hallé Orchestra in England, who was a boy of seven when Beethoven died.[1] The public funeral procession was one of the largest that Vienna had ever seen – schools were closed and an estimated twenty thousand people turned out.[2] In Franz Grillparzer's eulogy the poet spoke of Beethoven's achievements but also of his vulnerabilities, his deafness, and his alienation from society, all of which Grillparzer had witnessed during the 1820s when he had worked with Beethoven on an opera that never materialized. His funeral address, delivered by the actor Heinrich Anschütz, established some of the basic issues in Beethoven biography, issues that remained in the foreground for years afterward in mainstream commentary. The style of this oration was appropriately elevated and rhetorical, but through

[1] Charles Hallé, *The Autobiography of Charles Hallé, with Correspondence and Diaries*, ed. M. Kennedy (New York: Barnes & Noble, 1973), 28; quoted by Comini, *The Changing Image of Beethoven*, 74.

[2] For a thorough account of the funeral see Christopher Gibbs, "Vienna's Response to the Death of Beethoven," in *Beethoven and His World*, ed. Scott Burnham and Michael P. Steinberg (Princeton: Princeton University Press, 2000), 227–85.

it we can discern the main lines of Grillparzer's view of Beethoven:

> Standing by the grave of him who has passed away, we are in a manner the representatives of an entire nation, of the whole German people... The heir and amplifier of Handel's and Bach's, of Haydn's and Mozart's immortal fame is now no more... he was an artist, and all that was his, was his through art alone. The thorns of life had wounded him deeply, and as the castaway clings to the shore, so did he seek refuge in thine arms, O thou glorious sister and peer of the Good and the True...
>
> He was an artist but a man as well. A man in every sense – in the highest sense. Because he withdrew from the world they called him hostile, and because he held himself aloof from sentimentality, unfeeling... He fled the world because, in the depth of his loving nature, he found no foothold from which to oppose it. He withdrew from mankind because he had given them his all and received nothing in return. He dwelt alone, because he found no second self. But to the end of his life he had a loving heart for all men, a fatherly affection for his kindred, for all the world... Thus he was, thus he died, thus he will live to the end of time...[3]

What shines through is Grillparzer's view of Beethoven as a deaf and aloof genius, an alienated artist who was unable to find a lasting union with a woman (a "second self") but who yearned to reach out to "all the world." When we compare Grillparzer's language to that of other contemporaries who described their encounters with Beethoven, the same

[3] For a carefully edited text of Grillparzer's oration and related documents see Klaus Martin Kopitz and Rainer Cadenbach, eds., *Beethoven aus der Sicht seiner Zeitgenossen in Tagebüchern, Briefen, Gedichten und Erinnerungen* (Munich: G. Henle Verlag, 2009), 389–410.

themes often emerge. These themes have shaped an enduring portrait of Beethoven as both a totally committed artist
and a volatile, erratic, misanthropic personality. Where
many of these witnesses fall short, perhaps inevitably, is in
their inability to look below the surface to his subtlety and
depth as a human being, and to perceive the softer, intro-
spective and more complex aspects of his personality.

Contemporary Observers

From Beethoven's lifetime we possess a mass of miscel-
laneous observations by contemporaries who knew him
either at close range or at a distance. They include friends,
acquaintances, visitors, musicians, journalists, publishers,
and others who had known Beethoven in Bonn or during
his nearly thirty-five years in Vienna, and who left us verbal
accounts in their diaries, letters, poems, and memoirs, to
cite the headings in the title of the most recent publication
of all this material.[4] These observers, more than 250 of them,
are a heterogeneous group, ranging from Christian Gottlob
Neefe (Beethoven's boyhood teacher in Bonn) to the young
Franz Liszt (who reports having been brought to meet Beethoven in 1823 when he was eleven years old). Some of these
individuals also appear in Beethoven's correspondence or
as visitors writing messages in his Conversation Books, but
many recount their impressions of Beethoven when they
met him in his middle or later years.

A sample from among his acquaintances is the description by the English visitor Sir Julius Benedict, a pupil of Carl
Maria von Weber, who met Beethoven in Vienna in October

---

[4]   See fn. 3, the volumes were edited by Klaus Martin Kopitz and
Rainer Cadenbach, who passed away before its publication.

1823 and later described the meeting in a letter to Thayer of 1861.[5] Benedict remembered Beethoven as a

> stout, short man with a very red face, small, piercing eyes, and bushy eyebrows, dressed in a very long overcoat which reached nearly to his ankles... notwithstanding the high color of his cheeks and his general untidiness, there was in those small piercing eyes an expression which no painter could render. It was a feeling of sublimity and melancholy combined. I watched, as you can imagine, every word that he spoke when he took out his little book and began a conversation which to me, of course, was almost incomprehensible, inasmuch as he only answered questions pencilled to him by Messrs. Steiner and Haslinger [owners of a music shop and among Beethoven's publishers]...

> [And remembering a later meeting with Beethoven at Baden, Benedict describes] the wonderful impression his first appearance made on me was heightened every time I met him. When I saw him at Baden, his white hair flowing over his mighty shoulders, with that wonderful look – sometimes contracting his brows when anything afflicted him, sometimes bursting out into a forced laughter, indescribably painful to his listeners – I was touched as if King Lear or one of the old Gaelic bards stood before me...

It goes without saying that each contemporary brings his own sensitivities to his impressions of Beethoven, and what we have in this immense compilation is a vast array of descriptions that provided later biographers with raw material. Since we now possess complete and reliable editions of the original texts of Beethoven's letters and of the Conversation Books, the documentary material that is currently available greatly exceeds what could be accessed in earlier

5   Kopitz and Cadenbach, *Beethoven aus der Sicht*, 53–55; and TK III, 138ff.

times by even the most scrupulous writers. Accordingly, the traditional picture of Beethoven in his maturity – deaf, irascible, tramping through the streets of Vienna, heedless of his surroundings and utterly absorbed in his work – can be modified in various ways in the light of these contemporary reports, as modern biographers fill out their portrayals of Beethoven the man.

Early Attempts and Rivalries

A document dated 30 August 1826 and bearing Beethoven's signature gave the young Karl Holz authorization to write Beethoven's biography. Holz was then Beethoven's secretary and aide, as well as being second violinist of the Schuppanzigh Quartet, which he had joined in 1823.[6] The document (now in the Beethoven-Haus in Bonn) was more than likely written by Holz and merely signed by Beethoven. It probably resulted from conversations in which Beethoven felt enough trust in Holz to sign this statement, and it includes the curious remark that Holz "will not hand down to posterity in a garbled form the information which I have given him for that purpose." We have no way of knowing what

---

[6] For a thorough account of Holz's career see Hermann Ullrich, "Karl Holz, Beethovens letzter Freund," *Studien zur Musikwissenschaft*, 31 (1980), 67–189. For the 1826 document see the Beethoven-Haus website under "Letters," and for an English translation see Anderson III, Appendix No. 7. Although the German editors of the Conversation Books voiced doubts over the date of the document (*Konversationshefte*, Vol 10 (1993), 13), thinking it might have been forged by Holz in the early 1840s to support his rivalry with Schindler, these questions were resolved by Maynard Solomon *Beethoven*, (New York: Schirmer Books, 2nd edn, 1998), xviii, who showed that the hand of the document is consistent with that of Holz in the 1820s and that the stamped paper on which it was written was available in 1826.

"information" Beethoven might have given Holz, assuming that he gave him any at all, and there is no other testimony to show that he had actually selected Holz to be his "official" biographer. What is certain is that there were other claimants for this coveted role.

Late August of 1826 was an agonizing time for Beethoven, as we will see later in this book. In the previous months his nephew Karl's emotional and psychological struggles had increased to a breaking point. Eleven years earlier, in 1815, on the death of his brother Caspar Carl, Beethoven had begun his long legal battle to take over the guardianship of the nine-year-old Karl, arguing in the courts that Karl's mother Johanna was morally irresponsible and intellectually incapable of keeping her son with her. Over the years Karl had been the focus of continuing conflict between Beethoven and his sister-in-law, and the boy's education and potential for growth had surely been stunted by the turmoil of living with his eccentric, demanding, and deaf uncle, whom he also served as part-time copyist. By the summer of 1826 the tension had become unbearable. On August 5th Karl pawned his watch to buy a pistol, attempted suicide, wounded himself, was hospitalized and remained there until late September.[7]

In view of these tragic events in early August of 1826 it seems open to question as to whether, a few weeks later, Beethoven should have been thinking at leisure about who his eventual biographer might be. We know that at this time he was turning to Holz for help with many things, including Karl's affairs as well as his own, and as always he was deep in his current work (Opus 135 had just been begun in July). Accordingly, it looks as if Holz may have drafted this letter as a way of solidifying his role as Beethoven's trusted young assistant and to forestall claims by other would-be biographers, above all, Anton Schindler. Though Schindler

---

[7]   For the correct dating of Karl's attempt (not July 30 as often reported) see Solomon, *Beethoven*, 369 and 479 n. 32.

had been Beethoven's previous assistant for about two years, Beethoven had dismissed him after the concert of May 1824 at which the Ninth Symphony was premiered, and he had then been replaced by Holz.

Holz lived on until 1858 but never wrote the biography. He did, however, provide valuable information in conversations with some of the writers on Beethoven who were coming into view after 1840, among them the Russian critic Wilhelm von Lenz. In Lenz's *Beethoven: Eine Kunst-Studie* of 1860 he included comments in which Holz remembered Beethoven talking about aspects of the late quartets while they were still being conceived and written.[8] He also appears in the Conversation Books.

In 1843 Holz passed the "authorization document" of 30 August 1826 on to Ferdinand Simon Gassner, then the editor of a music journal – but with Gassner, too, the project came to nothing. Of course, by this time, in 1843, several Beethoven biographies were in print, and two of them – those by Wegeler-Ries and by Schindler – could lay claim to serious attention, whatever their individual merits.

Rivalries for priority in writing the first biography arose as early as 1827, and by the summer of that year the first one actually appeared. It was a short book by a Bohemian musician named Johann Aloys Schlosser, entitled *Ludwig van Beethoven: Eine Biographie*. The book was published in Prague with the date 1828, but was actually issued a year earlier.[9] Schindler despised it, and for once he was right,

[8] Wilhelm von Lenz, *Beethoven: Eine Kunst-Studie* (Hamburg: Hoffmann & Co., 1860), Part 5, 216–222. Lenz (p. 216) dates Holz's communications to him to 15 July 1857.

[9] In a letter to Moscheles of 14 September 1827, Schindler calls Schlosser's book "a truly miserable [*höchst miserable*] biography..." cited by Clemens Brenneis, "Das Fischhof Manuskript: Zur Frühgeschichte der Beethoven-Biographik," in *Zu Beethoven: Aufsätze und Annotationen*, ed. H. Goldschmidt (Berlin: Verlag Neue Musik, 1979), 90–116, at 112 n. 8. A translation of

as Schlosser's book is laced with factual errors and gives the impression of having been rushed into print so as to be the first in line.[10] It looks as if Schlosser, who worked in a Prague publishing house, was seizing the moment to glorify Beethoven and also the triumvirate of Haydn, Mozart, and Beethoven – but had only vague knowledge of what he was writing about.

During this same year, 1828, rumors were flying in Vienna that a new and trustworthy Beethoven biography was in the making, this one to be authored by Anton Gräffer, a member of the music-publishing firm of Artaria and Co.[11] Though Gräffer was not in Beethoven's inner circle – as Holz and Schindler had been, at least for some periods of time – he apparently had support from Jakob Hotschevar, who had become the guardian of nephew Karl in June 1827 after the death of Beethoven's old friend Stephan von Breuning. As Brenneis points out, this Vienna biography project was meant not only to honor Beethoven's memory but also to reflect the broad feeling of Austrian national pride in his accomplishments.

Schlosser's book was issued as *Beethoven: the First Biography*, edited by Barry Cooper and translated by Reinhard G. Pauly (Portland: Amadeus Press, 1996). Cooper's introduction is a useful review of the book, its feeble merits and many short-comings. Among various other negative assessments see Kristin Knittel, "Imitation, Individuality, and Illness: Beethoven's Three Styles," *BF* 4, 21ff.

[10] Curiously Schlosser announces on his title page that his aim was to raise money for a monument to Haydn, about whom he also intended to write a biography. This never appeared but in 1828 he did bring out a short biography of Mozart.

[11] Brenneis, "Das Fischhof Manuskript," 90–103. A valuable excerpt from Gräffer's memoirs was published by Rita Steblin, "Reminiscences of Beethoven in Anton Gräffer's unpublished memoirs: a legacy of the Viennese biography project of 1827," *BBS* 4 (2005), 149–89.

In the meantime, Anton Schindler, who was certain that he alone could write the only legitimate biography, nursed his plans with the same intensity with which he slandered others who had been close to Beethoven, including Holz and Beethoven's brother Johann. Schindler apparently fabricated a scenario in which Beethoven, near the end of his life, had allegedly asked Friedrich Rochlitz (the founding editor of the *Allgemeine Musikalischer Zeitung*) to write his biography and that Rochlitz ultimately declined on grounds of his poor health, leaving the task to Schindler.[12]

Schindler's campaign also included his contacts with Franz Wegeler (an early friend of Beethoven's in the Bonn years and later also in Vienna before he returned to the Rhineland). Wegeler generously provided Schindler with personal documents, believing that this was a worthy project. But Wegeler soon became disillusioned with Schindler after making contact with Ferdinand Ries, his loyal friend from Bonn, who was a distinguished pianist and composer as well as having been a former pupil of Beethoven's. Wegeler and Ries now made plans to collaborate on a volume of memoirs about Beethoven. The book that resulted, however short and limited in scope, became the first classic in the literature of Beethoven biography.

Wegeler and Ries, 1838

The *Biographische Notizen über Ludwig van Beethoven*, co-authored by Franz Wegeler and Ferdinand Ries, was published at Koblenz in 1838, a few months after Ries's death in January of that year. Seven years later, in 1845, when the Beethoven statue in Bonn was displayed for the first time, Wegeler published an appendix to the volume that is both a continuation and a personal tribute to Ries, whom he calls his "unforgettable friend." Wegeler explains that as old

---

[12] On this tale see Brenneis, "Das Fischhof Manuskript," 95ff.

friends who had known Beethoven over his lifetime, their aim had been to record their memories and correct "errors and false statements" that had begun to abound. Surely, in 1845, he had Schindler in mind.

In fact, Wegeler-Ries, as it came to be known, should be read not only as a labor of love but as a corrective to the other attempts at biography that had surfaced from 1827 on. One aspect of their work that commands respect is that both men had known Beethoven personally and had memories that went back to his early years. As natives of Bonn they could see Beethoven not only as a great European composer, a world figure, but as a fellow Rhinelander who came from their own home town and with whom they had grown up. Their personal backgrounds sharply distinguish them from all the other earlier biographers or would-be biographers – including Holz and Schindler – who knew Beethoven only in Vienna and only in his later years, when he was deaf, irascible, and immersed within his inner world.

Franz Wegeler (1765–1848) had studied medicine in Bonn and then in Vienna, and taught at the university in Bonn from 1789 to 1794, when the French invasion caused him to flee to Vienna for several years until he returned to Bonn in 1796. In 1802 he married Eleonore von Breuning, a member of the family in Bonn who had befriended the young Beethoven in his early years, and to whom Beethoven himself had been attracted in the early 1790s. Wegeler's later years of medical practice were at Koblenz, on the Rhine. But his early friendship with Beethoven not only lasted but meant a good deal to Beethoven. It was to Wegeler that he wrote a letter in 1801 in which he revealed his deafness and his fear of its consequences, and it was to Wegeler that Beethoven wrote in December 1826, within a few months of his death, to record his memories of their childhood friendship: "If we drifted apart, that was due to the nature of our lives… yet the eternally unshakable foundations of what is good always held us strongly together... my beloved friend..."[13]

As for Ferdinand Ries (1784–1838), he was the son of Franz Ries, a leading musician at Bonn, and, with Czerny, among the very few Beethoven pupils who forged his own successful career as a composer and pianist. The special value of Ries's memoirs lies in his having been closely associated with Beethoven in 1801–05 and 1808–09, that is, in two important segments of the great middle period of Beethoven's artistic life. We are struck by Ries's candor in reporting episodes in Beethoven's life to which he was an eye-witness. As Tyson says, they have a "special kind of pictorial vividness."[14] They include his description of a walk with Beethoven in the countryside, probably around 1802 or 1803, in which they heard a shepherd playing a flute, but Beethoven

> could hear nothing for half an hour, and though I repeatedly assured him that I could no longer hear anything (which however was not the case) he became extraordinary quiet and gloomy. [15]

Ries's career – in Vienna, Paris, later in London and finally in Bonn and Frankfurt – brought him recognition as a prolific composer, pianist, and conductor. In 1825 he conducted the Ninth Symphony at a festival at Aix-la-Chapelle, and with characteristic generosity of spirit he wrote to

---

[13] *Briefwechsel*, No. 2236; Anderson No. 1542; see also my *Beethoven:The Music and the Life*, 12.

[14] Alan Tyson, "Ferdinand Ries (1784–1838): the History of His Contribution to Beethoven Biography," *19th-Century Music*, 2/3 (1984), 220.

[15] Franz Gerhard Wegeler and Ferdinand Ries, *Beethoven Remembered*, translated by Frederick Noonan (Arlington VA: Great Ocean Publishers, 1987); translation slightly modified here.

Beethoven to say that this monumental work, then still new to the world, "is without its equal, and if you had written nothing but this, you would have made yourself immortal. Where will you lead us from here?"[16]

Gerhard von Breuning

Gerhard von Breuning (1813–92) holds a special place among contemporaries who knew Beethoven, above all because he was a boy of twelve in 1825 when Beethoven moved into the *Schwarzspanierhaus* (the House of the Black-Robed Spaniards), near the building in which the family of Stephan von Breuning, Gerhard's father, then lived. Stephan had been a childhood friend of Beethoven's in Bonn, had moved to Vienna in the 1790s and remained there for many years as a government employee. His relationship with Beethoven suffered ups and downs, but when the aging composer became his neighbor in the summer of 1825 they resumed their old friendship. From mid-1825 to March 1827, when Beethoven died, they were on familiar terms – that is, not only Stephan but his young son Gerhard as well. In later years it was Gerhard who wrote vivid recollections of that poignant time when he was a fairly frequent visitor to Beethoven and gained his paternal affection (Beethoven called him by pet names, including "Ariel," from *The Tempest*). Gerhard saw Beethoven in his daily life, observed his turbulent relationship with nephew Karl and others, and witnessed his last illness, from December 1826 to the end. Many years later, in 1874, Gerhard published his memoir of that period, with the title *Aus dem Schwarzspanierhaus* ("From the House of the

---

[16] For Ries's letter see T. Albrecht, ed., *Letters to Beethoven and Other Correspondence*, 3 vols. (Lincoln NE and London: University of Nebraska Press, 1996–7) No. 409, dated 9 June 1825. For an excellent introduction to Wegeler-Ries and the early rivalries among biographers see Tyson, "Ferdinand Ries," 209–21, especially 210ff.

Black-Robed Spaniards"), and in its vividness and directness of observation it is of special importance, the more so since it shows us the aging composer with both his appealing and eccentric personal qualities rolled into one.

As Maynard Solomon pointed out in his translation of the volume, Gerhard "does not quote from his own entries in the conversation books, [but] the general tenor of his recollections is often confirmed by the surviving conversations."[17] Gerhard's descriptions are often highly personal and revealing, and his testimony deserves credence, above all in comparison to Schindler, whose fabrications became known only much later. And as Solomon points out, we should also remember that in 1874, when Gerhard published this memoir, "neither Thayer's nor Nohl's biographies, though their publications commenced in the 1860s, had yet reached Beethoven's final decade..."[18] It is also worth noting that, unlike Holz, Schindler, and the other would-be biographers in the early phase of this literature, Gerhard von Breuning had no thought whatever of imagining himself as a Beethoven authority but simply reports what he personally observed up close in this last period of Beethoven's life.

[17] Gerhard von Breuning, *Memories of Beethoven: From the House of the Black-Robed Spaniards,* translated by Henry Mins and Maynard Solomon from von Breuning's *Aus dem Schwarzspanierhaus* (Cambridge: Cambridge University Press, 1992).

[18] Editor's introduction to von Breuning, *Memories of Beethoven,* 5.

2

Beethoven Biography, 1840–c. 1875

❧

The Emergence of Beethoven Biography

I N 1838 THE PUBLICATION of Wegeler and Ries's *Biographische Notizen* opened up the world of Beethoven biography and commentary. It spurred others to plan their own entries into the field, whether they framed their work as essays, personal reminiscences, or longer and more ambitious accounts of the composer's life and works. In this newly competitive atmosphere Anton Schindler needed no encouragement, and he characteristically puffed his own importance by denigrating Ferdinand Ries as a trustworthy writer on Beethoven, an attitude which Ries reciprocated.[1]

By about 1840, the image of Beethoven as a central cultural figure was already established, not only in Germany but across Europe and in America, and biographical and critical commentaries began to proliferate. It is hardly surprising that the two dimensions were often intertwined, a feature that has continued down to our own time, of course in successively changing contexts. The more rigorous side of the critical literature developed in the growing discipline of musical analysis, which tended to separate itself off from biography and, depending on the analyst, from criticism, a separation that began in the late 19th and early 20th centuries and continues to prevail.

---

[1] See Daniel Brenner, *Anton Schindler und sein Einfluss auf die Beethoven-Biographik* (Bonn: Beethoven-Haus, 2013), 70ff.

A very few mid-19th-century Beethoven biographers, above all Thayer, rigorously pursued historical and biographical issues, while others, notably Wilhelm von Lenz and Adolph Bernhard Marx, focused mainly on the works. Lenz and Marx included some biographical material in their published works but neither one controlled the facts at Thayer's level, as he did not hesitate to point out in his reviews. In 1840 Anton Schindler took the stage as the most self-promoting of all current biographers. His *Biographie von Ludwig van Beethoven* was published in that year, followed in 1842 by his *Beethoven in Paris* and by later editions of his biography in 1845 and 1860.[2] It continued to influence later biographers for many decades, though not without occasional criticisms. Even as late as 1966, when the first modern English translations of Schindler appeared, edited and annotated by the painstaking Beethoven scholar, Donald MacArdle, neither he nor anyone thought to question Schindler's claim to have been a close confidante of Beethoven's for many years.[3] And until the 1970s, when Schindler's tampering with primary sources began to be revealed, writers on Beethoven were

---

[2] For a chronology of Schindler's writings see the English translation by Donald W. MacArdle, *Beethoven as I Knew Him* (Chapel Hill: University of North Carolina Press, 1966), 29f.

[3] See especially Brenner, *Schindler*, Chapter 4 on Schindler's lasting influence on German Beethoven biographies of Beethoven. Among the writers whom Brenner singles out for their discussions of Schindler, including criticism and corrections of facts, are Thayer, Nottebohm, Ludwig Nohl, Bekker, Riezler, and Schmitz. Also discussed are later editors of Schindler's biography, including Alfred Kalischer (1909) and Fritz Volbach (1927), and an article by Walther Nohl (1925). See Theodore Albrecht, "Anton Schindler as Destroyer and Forger of Beethoven's Conversation Books: A Case for Decriminalization," in *Music's Intellectual History*, ed. Zdravko Blažeković and Barbara Dobbs Mackenzie (New York: *RILM*, 2009), 169–181; also Brenner, *Schindler*, 12–14.

unaware of his forgeries in the conversation books or his other questionable actions as historian and biographer.

If we leave aside a raft of journal articles and other relevant volumes that appeared after 1840 – such as partial collections of Beethoven's letters or the many *feuilletons* written to celebrate the Beethoven monument erected in Bonn in 1845 – we can focus on the more substantial early biographies and other books that contributed to public knowledge of his life and works.

For the period from 1840 to 1870 my short list of important publications that are mainly biographies or include some valuable biographical material, is as follows:

Anton Schindler, *Biographie von Ludwig von Beethoven* (and later editions, down to 1860)

Anton Schindler, *Beethoven in Paris*

Wilhelm von Lenz, *Beethoven et ses trois styles*

Wilhelm von Lenz, *Beethoven: Eine Kunst-Studie*

A. B. Marx, *Ludwig van Beethoven: Leben und Schaffen*

Ludwig Nohl, *Beethovens Leben*

Alexander Wheelock Thayer, *Chronologisches Verzeichnis der Werke Ludwig van Beethoven*

Gustav Nottebohm, *Ein Skizzenbuch von Beethoven* [Nottebohm's first major publication, on Beethoven's "Kessler" Sketch book of 1802].

Thayer-Deiters, *Ludwig van Beethovens Leben*, Vol. 1

Nottebohm, *Thematisches Verzeichnis der im Druck erschienen Werke von Ludwig van Beethoven*

Richard Wagner, *Beethoven* (not biographical but a major critical essay; see below for Wagner's abortive idea to collaborate in the writing of a Beethoven biography in 1841)

Among these writers I distinguish a principal group whose work carried authority by demonstrating true biographical insights – they are Wegeler and Ries, to some extent Schindler (within the limits we have now come to recognize), Thayer, and, in a special sense, Nottebohm. I contrast their work with those of a secondary group – Lenz, Marx, and Nohl – who broke new ground in offering critical appraisals of Beethoven's works to a broad public, and indeed were widely read and reprinted, but have not remained influential down to modern times. In the portraits that follow I will discuss the contributions of Schindler, Thayer, and Nottebohm, and then offer short appraisals of the other writers whose work appeared between 1850 and 1870. They will mainly appear in approximately chronological order, except for Richard Wagner, who inevitably demands special treatment in any work on Beethoven commentary.

Anton Schindler as Biographer and Falsifier, 1840–60

In 1840, with the publication of his *Biographie von Ludwig van Beethoven*, in two parts, including a portrait of Beethoven and four facsimiles, Anton Schindler (1795–1864) stepped forward before the world as, apparently, the reigning authority on the life and times of Beethoven.[4] Within a year his book was translated into English by the pianist Ignaz Moscheles, who was enjoying a successful career in England, and the *Life of Beethoven*, with Moscheles's notes but curiously without Schindler's name on the title page, appeared in London in 1841.[5] Covering his tracks with some skill and cleverness, Schindler let it appear in his book that he had

---

[4]   In the light of recent revelations about Schindler's trustworthiness, an important contribution is Albrecht's article of 2009, "Anton Schindler as Destroyer ...," (see above, n. 3). On Schindler as man and writer see Brenner, *Schindler.*

[5]   On Moscheles's translation and his difficulties with Schindler see Mark Kroll, *Ignaz Moscheles and the Changing World of Musical Europe* (Woodbridge: Boydell Press, 2014), especially 234–8.

been intimately associated with Beethoven for many years, from at latest 1816 until his death in 1827. In fact, he had probably played the violin in some of Beethoven's concerts of 1814 and may have casually encountered him when Schindler was working as a clerk in the office of Beethoven's lawyer, Johann Baptist Bach.[6] But his claim to having been a truly close associate of the composer for almost ten years was a falsehood that was accepted for more than a century by even the most scrupulous Beethoven scholars, as we will see.

The truth is that Schindler's unpaid service with Beethoven lasted less than two years, from the fall of 1822 until the end of May 1824, when their relationship broke down over money, specifically the proceeds from the Ninth Symphony premiere that had taken place in that month.[7] Schindler had served as a man of all work, doing errands and undertaking tasks for Beethoven who, however, disliked and distrusted him well before the rupture in 1824. In a letter of summer 1823 to his brother Johann, Beethoven described Schindler as a "miserable scoundrel," and just three days earlier, in a loving letter to his nephew Karl, Beethoven had told Karl that "I do not care to have any direct association with that miserable fellow…[8]

It was after Schindler's dismissal that Karl Holz came on the scene as Beethoven's new assistant, beginning about July of 1825 and lasting until December 1826, three months before Beethoven's death. Why Holz withdrew from close contact in the final months is not clear, but it was then that Schindler reappeared, no doubt sensing that in this time of

6   I am indebted here to Theodore Albrecht for his close reading of my discussion of Schindler.

7   On the dates of Schindler's service with Beethoven see Albrecht, "Anton Schindler as Destroyer…," 173, and more fully detailed in Brenner, *Schindler*, 11–23.

8   Letter to brother Johann of 19 August 1823: *Briefwechsel* 1731; Anderson 1231; to Karl on 16 August 1823; *Briefwechsel* 1728; Anderson 1230.

Beethoven's decline and final illness he could try to establish a position of prominence in Beethoven's intimate circle and look to the future as an eye-witness and spokesman.[9]

After Beethoven's death, which was of course a major cultural event, a spate of short journal articles appeared with reminiscences or commentaries on the music. They included Ignaz von Seyfried's personal recollections of Beethoven, attached to his 1832 edition of Beethoven's counterpoint studies, a hapless effort that was later revised by Nottebohm.[10] But the only personal memoirs of real value published in these years were the *Biographische Notizen* by Wegeler and Ries in 1838. Still, their short volume had never been intended to be a comprehensive "life," which Schindler now, in 1840, published proudly for the first time.

In 1842 Schindler kept up the pace with a new essay entitled *Beethoven in Paris*, based on his visit to Paris in 1841 but adding a biographical supplement and a facsimile of Beethoven's handwriting. Then came a second edition of his *Biographie* in 1845. In 1860 he brought out the "third, newly revised and extended edition," now with a foreword in which Schindler announced that this third edition was "much expanded and supplemented," with extended commentary and with many dates corrected. In this 1860 foreword he also went to some trouble to comment on his rivals, including Wegeler and especially Ries (whom he openly disliked and now falsely impugned as having had a "long-cherished grudge in his heart against his friend and teacher"). And

---

9   Peter Clive, *Beethoven and His World: A Biographical Dictionary* (Oxford: Oxford University Press, 2001), 169, speculates that there had been some estrangement between Holz and Beethoven, perhaps over a quarrel and in view of Holz's engagement to marry Elisabeth von Bogner, as he did in May 1827.

10 On Seyfried's publication and Nottebohm's revised edition of 1873 see Julia Ronge, *Beethovens Lehrzeit: Kompositionsstudien bei Joseph Haydn, Johann Georg Albrechtsberger und Antonio Salieri* (Bonn: Beethoven-Haus, 2011).

he also took the occasion to demean other writers on Beethoven, including Wilhelm von Lenz and A. B. Marx. Lenz's *Beethoven et ses Trois Styles* had come out in 1852, followed in 1855 by his *Beethoven: Eine Kunst-Studie* – both of them wide-ranging critical appraisals of Beethoven's works. Schindler brushed aside the biographical portion of Lenz's 1855 volume with the claim that it "is nothing but a rehash of the biographical section of my book", and said of Marx's *Beethoven, Leben und Schaffen* (1859) that he too made "no less comprehensive use of my book…" though he did give Marx credit for musical insights.[11]

Schindler's low opinion of his contemporaries who had known Beethoven was reciprocated. A telling sample is a comment by Ferdinand Hiller, a gifted musician and student of Hummel's, who had been with Hummel at Beethoven's bedside during his last illness. In his later reminiscences Hiller offered this extraordinary view of him:

> The fact that this sublime master could associate daily with this knight of the sorrowful countenance for a number of years, and had not turned him out, can only be explained by the fact that at that time he was indifferent to the outside world and needed an intelligent servant. I do not deny that Schindler had some knowledge of music and some intellectual ability, but his personality was as spare as his figure and as dry as his facial expression. Certainly he was of service to Beethoven in many ways, and it is just as certain that no friendship was ever exploited more cleverly and to greater advantage.

[11] Schindler, foreword to the 1860 edition. For his remarks on Lenz and Marx I am quoting from MacArdle's translation, p. 28f. Further comments on Marx appear throughout the 1860 edition, with Schindler always presenting himself in his role as eye-witness; e.g, p. 130 on the *Leonore* overtures: "If only Marx could have spent a week in Beethoven's company and heard him talk!"

In later years, when Schindler was visited by a music lover whom he wanted to honor or especially please, he would appear wearing an unattractive dressing gown which Beethoven had once worn threadbare, thus presenting, without realizing it, a highly accurate picture of his relationship to the great man who had merely tolerated him.[12]

The image of Schindler wearing Beethoven's worn-out dressing gown speaks volumes about his pathological belief that he was destined to be the true posthumous representative of Beethoven, and his later forgeries and misrepresentations go hand in hand with the portrait depicted by Hiller. In a letter to Wegeler of 20 June 1828, a little more than a year after Beethoven's death, Schindler had described his feeling of virtual disbelief that Beethoven was actually dead. He goes on to write as follows:

...Above my writing desk hangs his portrait... under it hangs his profession of faith, written out in his own hand, which he always had on his writing desk.[13] Around it are his beloved books, from which he always read, and the notes he made about them... and his walking stick and compass, with which he made all his excursions; his candlestick; his coffee machine, in which he made his own coffee for 8–9 years, always making it himself and

---

[12] The full original text is given in Daniel Brenner, *Schindler*, 156. My translation differs slightly from that in George Barth, *The Pianist as Orator. Beethoven and the Transformation of Keyboard Style*. (Ithaca NY: Cornell University Press, 1992), 68f., citing an earlier version by Eva Badura-Skoda.

[13] The reference is to Beethoven's "Glaubensbekenntnis," consisting of quotations from Schiller's *Die Sendung Moses*. On this document and its background see Friederike Grigat, *Beethovens Glaubensbekenntnis: Drei Denksprüche aus Friedrich Schillers Aufsatz Die Sendung Moses*, (Bonn: Beethoven-Haus Verlag, 2008).

also for his guests; his gray robe, the one in which he is portrayed by Stieler while writing the *Missa Solemnis...* and many other papers and manuscripts... All these, not priceless memorials in themselves, are so much the more dear to me because he had a special love for them... you can easily imagine how much I am still occupied with my loving friend[14]

It is as if Schindler were in a delusional state in which he imagines himself as Beethoven's true heir, the faithful guardian of the heritage – and it is not far-fetched to imagine him in later years sitting down to write forged entries into pages of the Conversation Books while wearing the gray robe that had belonged to Beethoven.[15]

In these years, from 1830 to 1860, we are in the high tide of German musical romanticism. It is the period of the maturity of Mendelssohn and Schumann and of Berlioz, Chopin, and Liszt; the time of Wagner's early romantic operas and his immense development that reached its first culmination in *Tristan* (1859). From 1850 on, it is the period of the early keyboard works and chamber music of Brahms, along with the transformations of musical style and ethos that were being felt in France, England, Russia, and elsewhere. The German musical world was now becoming sharply divided between what Franz Brendel called the "New German School," which promoted Wagner, Liszt, and Berlioz as the "progressive"

---

14 For the letter see Brenner, *Schindler*, 59.
15 A touching parallel was pointed out to me by my wife, Ava Bry Penman, herself a former student of Anna Freud. As described by Elisabeth Young-Bruehl in her biography of Anna Freud, in her last days the daughter of Sigmund Freud "sat wrapped inside her father's big wool coat." See Elisabeth Young-Bruehl, *Anna Freud: A Biography* (New York: Summit Books, 1988), 453.

composers for whom program music and music drama were
the newly significant genres, standing in opposition to the
conservative group, including Brahms and Joachim, who
signed a manifesto in 1860 that argued against "the so-called
music of the future" and implicitly for the continued vitality
of traditional forms of instrumental music.[16] The paradox
was that both sides could claim Beethoven as their major
forebear and artistic model.

Accordingly, the Beethoven myth, already well established, was now being magnified, and he was now revered as
the towering master who had shown the way to all that was
new and important in the world of music. The monument
raised to Beethoven in Bonn in 1845 was only the most visible symbol of his stature as the god of music for composers,
performers, and the world at large.

And so Schindler's biographical portrait, the first in the
field, remained influential, especially in German musical
circles, despite the emergence of younger rivals, among
them Alexander Wheelock Thayer, who began to challenge
him on facts and dates as well as on broad interpretative
matters. Yet Schindler's claim to having been a ten-year
eye-witness to Beethoven actually withstood its challenges
firmly enough for a century and more. As late as the 1950s a
dictionary article on him could say that "his intimacy with
Beethoven lends peculiar value to his *Biographie*..."[17] In the
1960s Donald MacArdle, a devoted and assiduous Beethoven scholar, published a complete English translation of

[16] See Carl Dahlhaus, *Nineteenth-Century Music*, trans. J. Brad-
     ford Robinson (Berkeley: University of California Press, 1989)
     252f; and for the manifesto, Christian Martin Schmidt, *Jo-
     hannes Brahms und Seine Zeit*, (Laaber: Laaber-Verlag, 1998)
     20f.

[17] *Baker's Biographical Dictionary of Musicians*, Fifth edition, ed.
     Nicolas Slonimsky (New York: G. Schirmer, 1958), 1438f.

Schindler's biography entitled *Beethoven as I Knew Him*.[18] This translation came out in 1966, not long after MacArdle's death in December 1964. In his Editor's Foreword, MacArdle wrote:

> Anton Schindler is the one author who could appropriately have written a book entitled *Beethoven As I Knew Him*. For most of the last ten years of the composer's life, Schindler was intimately associated with him: as pupil, as scrivener and servant, sometimes almost as factotum, sometimes almost as member of the family.[19]

Although his translation is well supplied with useful editorial notes, some of which correct dates and details in Schindler's text, neither MacArdle nor anyone else in 1964 could know that a few years later Schindler's forged entries in the Conversation Books would be revealed and that his claim to have been associated closely with Beethoven over ten years and more would be generally dismissed as a fabrication.

And so in the 1970s Schindler's reputation collapsed. The story began with the Beethoven conversation books, the little notebooks in which Beethoven's visitors and others had written down their side of their conversations with the deaf composer from 1818 to 1827.[20] Schindler had obtained these books from Stephan von Breuning, who had also been a regular witness during Beethoven's last illness and had become nephew Karl's guardian, but who himself died only two months after Beethoven. When von Breuning passed along the body of the conversation books to Schindler there were not four hundred of them, as was sometimes later

---

[18] Anton Schindler, *Beethoven As I Knew Him*. (Chapel Hill: University of North Carolina Press, 1966). It contains lengthy annotations by MacArdle that are of value.

[19] *Ibid.*, 19.

[20] For a recent study of Beethoven's deafness see Robin Wallace, *Hearing Beethoven: A Story of Musical Loss and Discovery* (Chicago: University of Chicago Press, 2018).

believed, but many more than a hundred – the surviving total was and is 139 conversation books.[21]

In January 1846 Schindler sold the whole collection and other important material to the Prussian Royal Library in Berlin, where from then on others could consult them – among them Thayer, in the early stages of his own biography project. In modern times, attempts to publish the conversation books began in the 1920s, and a transcription of the first five years of their contents came out in Germany in 1941–43, despite wartime conditions. Between 1968 and 2001 a reliable edition of the whole set was published in eleven volumes, edited by a team of scholars headed by Karl-Heinz Köhler with Dagmar Beck and Grita Herre, with copious annotations.[22] A complete English translation by Theodore Albrecht, newly annotated, has begun to appear in 2018.[23]

In the 1970s the English critic Peter Stadlen, then working on the problem of Beethoven's metronome markings, noticed that there were many entries in these little books that Schindler had added in originally empty spaces and on pages that had been left blank. Meantime, Dagmar Beck and Grita Herre systematically identified many more of Schindler's

[21] On the number of books and the circumstances of their preservation see Albrecht, "Anton Schindler as Destroyer ...," especially 173–181. For a recent summary of Schindler's insertions and falsifications in the conversation books see Brenner, *Schindler*, 23–36, and the articles by Stadlen and by Herre and Beck cited in notes 24 and 26. For the correct number of the conversation books and the reason why the number "four hundred" went into circulation, see AlbrechtBC, Volume 1, xv.

[22] *Ludwig van Beethovens Konversationshefte*, ed. Karl-Heinz Köhler with Grita Herre and Dagmar Beck (Leipzig: VEB Deutscher Verlag für Musik), 11 volumes, 1968–2001.

[23] AlbrechtBC. For a review of the publication history of the Beethoven Conversation Books, see Albrecht, "Anton Schindler as Destroyer...," 169–181 and especially nn. 1 and 2.

forgeries, saw that their orthography corresponded to Schindler's hand in documents written after 1827, and submitted all the evidence to specialists in criminal forgery cases, who confirmed their findings. They also published facsimiles of Schindler's handwriting before and after 1827 that bear out their claims.[24] In that same year, 1977, they published an extensive list of 150 false entries that Schindler had created while the books were in his possession.[25]

Schindler had artfully designed these insertions to look authentic, and those that he added to already written-on pages were often concocted to fit in with the topics that were under discussion when the pages were first inscribed by Beethoven's visitors. In some instances Schindler used a blank page to write a whole series of fictitious exchanges with Beethoven, often choosing topics on which Schindler had pet theories, such as the proper tempi for performance and metronome marks. All this was meant to bolster Schindler's claim that he had been a close confidant of Beethoven's during his last years. A typical false entry dated February 1827 (a month before Beethoven's death) reads as follows:

> ...I will not be like Ries. What you have taught me will not be suppressed in the world and my highest goal will be to bring it to others, as you have instructed me to do.[26]

[24] Dagmar Beck and Grita Herre, "Einige Zweifel an der Überlieferung der Konversationshefte," in *Bericht über den Internationalen Beethoven-Kongress Berlin 1977* (Leipzig: VEB DeutscherVerlag fur Musik, 1978), pp. 257–69. For six facsimile illustrations of Schindler's handwriting before and after 1827, see. pp. 270–74.

[25] Dagmar Beck and Grita Herre, "Anton Schindler's fingierte Eintragungen in den Konversationsheften," in Harry Goldschmidt, ed. *Zu Beethoven: Aufsätze und Annotationen* (Berlin: Verlag Neue Musik, 1979), Vol. 1, 11–89.

[26] Herre and Beck, "Überlieferung der Konversationshefte," 87. Peter Stadlen, "Schindler's Beethoven Forgeries," *The Musical Times* 118/7 (July 1977), 256–52 (and other articles). My

Other false entries included a canon on "Ta-ta-ta-ta," etc., which Schindler ascribed to Beethoven but evidently wrote himself and proposed as a precursor to the slow movement of the Eighth Symphony, with its repeated notes at the beginning.[27] Another interesting and influential entry, which Schindler added to a conversation book of 1823 reads as follows:

"Zwei Principe auch im Mittelsatz der Pathetique"

"Tausende fassen das nicht"

["Two principles also in the middle movement of the Pathétique sonata" and, after Beethoven's alleged reply, Schindler continues: "Thousands don't grasp that."]

In 1923 the Beethoven scholar Arnold Schmitz wrote an influential book based on this entry, entitled *Beethovens Zwei Prinzipe* ("Beethoven's Two Principles"), a study of thematic contrasts and thematic derivation in Beethoven's instrumental works.[28] Of course, Schmitz could know nothing of Schindler's false entries, and as a critical study his book can still be read with profit. But the documentary point of origin on which he based the book was a Schindler forgery.

Schindler possessed other important Beethoven manuscripts, including the autograph scores and corrected copies of several works, two large-format sketchbooks and a number of pocket sketchbooks – all of which he sold to the

---

quotations from Schindler's false entries here come from the comprehensive listing of all of them in Beck and Herre, "Anton Schindlers fingierte Eintragungen in den Konversationsheften". See also Helga Lühning, "Das Schindler und das Beethoven-Bild," *BBS* 2 (2001), 183–200 and especially 184.

[27] See LvBWV, Vol. 2, 672f. where it is listed under doubtful works as WoO 162.

[28] Arnold Schmitz, *Beethovens Zwei Prinzipe: ihre Bedeutung für Themen- und Satzbau*, (Berlin: Dümmlers Verlagsbuchhand-lung, 1923).

Berlin library in 1846.[29] There is good evidence that Schindler subjected some of them to the same treatment that he gave to the conversation books. In 1827, when he presented a pocket sketchbook to Ignaz Moscheles, he removed the first gathering. Also, several sketch leaves inscribed by Schindler found their way into other collections of sketches; and, as Douglas Johnson puts it, in some cases he "inked over pencilled entries in both the conversation books and the sketchbooks."[30]

Still, when all is said and done regarding Schindler's fraudulent additions to the conversation books, some of which became incorporated into his biography, questions remain. Is it possible that some of Schindler's entries might not have been wholly invented, but might have been based on remarks he could recall from conversations with Beethoven during his months of close association with him, from autumn of 1822 to spring of 1824? The same question haunts his biography in its various editions. Schindler's pathetic and overwhelming urge to portray himself as Beethoven's true spokesman, who could literally wear his robe, despising so many others who had known Beethoven, clearly ruined his judgment and common sense. He presented himself as the "ami de Beethoven," a title that he had engraved on his visiting card, as Heinrich Heine wrote in a withering description of "this dark beanpole of a man, with a horrible white tie and a funereal expression."[31] We can only wonder whether, in the

[29] For a thorough account of the Beethoven manuscripts in Schindler's possession after Beethoven's death see JTW, 40f. ("The Schindler Collection").

[30] *Ibid.*, p. 41. See also Robert Winter's review of the Beethoven-Haus edition of the Wittgenstein sketchbook (edited by J. Schmidt-Görg, Bonn: Verlag des Beethovenhauses, 1968–1972) in *JAMS* 28,1 (1975), 135–38.

[31] Frequently quoted, e,g, in H. Lühning, "Das Schindler und das Beethoven-Bild," *BBS* 2 (2001), 193, and in Brenner, *Schindler*, 84.

moment when Schindler sold all the conversation books to the Berlin library and thus released them to posterity, it might have dimly occurred to him that, some day, ardent sleuths might uncover his falsifications and his corruption of valuable historical evidence.

The exposure of Schindler's mendacity is not a trivial matter for Beethoven historiography, since he created a portrait of Beethoven that lasted for a very long time. Some of his anecdotes and comments are among the most frequently quoted in the literature. We should remember that he probably added many of these false entries into the conversation books during the very years in which he was preparing his biography, and after it came out in 1840 he may well have continued to insert them into these pages as long as he possessed these books – that is to say, up to January 1846. At the very least, we have to approach his testimony concerning Beethoven with extreme caution when there is no corroboration from other sources – which is often the case. In late 1822, when Schindler came on the scene, Beethoven was in the thick of work on the Ninth Symphony and was trying to publish and distribute manuscript copies of the *Missa Solemnis*. It was then that Beethoven returned to the completion of the Diabelli Variations (April 1823) and other projects. To whatever extent Schindler's reporting of Beethoven's comments – on virtually anything – could be authentic, they would belong to that period.

Schindler does not rank with famous art forgers such as Han van Meegeren, who made false Vermeer paintings, or literary miscreants such as William Henry Ireland and John Payne Collier, who created false documents about Shakespeare.[32] But in music history Schindler counts as the

---

[32] On these Shakespeare forgers see Samuel Schoenbaum, *Shakespeare's Lives*, New Edition (Oxford: Oxford University Press, 1991), 132–6 etc. on Ireland and 245–66 on Collier; and James

prime example of a witness and biographer whose yearning for fame took possession of him and led him over the edge. And so it is a remarkable feature of Beethoven biography that one of its founding fathers should turn out to have been an unscrupulous forger of documents whose work never-theless remained influential for more than a century after his biography first appeared in print.

Alexander Wheelock Thayer and the Pursuit of Truth: His Earlier Work, 1849–66

Establishing a thorough and accurate portrait of Beethoven's life in the wake of Schindler's highly colored biography and the romantic tales spun by other admirers became the life-long mission of Alexander Wheelock Thayer (1817–97). By doing so, Thayer became the true founding father of modern Beethoven biography.[33] Thayer's achievement reflected his unusual personal qualities, his grasp of the need for histor-ical and biographical truth and his tenacity in searching for the sources that would reveal it. It must also have stemmed from his awareness of the importance of Beethoven in Europe and America in these years.

Shapiro, *Contested Will: Who Wrote Shakespeare* (New York: Simon and Schuster, 2010), 32–36 etc. on Ireland, and 64f. on Collier.

[33] Recent valuable publications on Thayer are by Grant William Cook, in articles in *The Beethoven Journal* from 2002 to the present. For Cook's conspectus of Thayer's career, see his "Al-exander Wheelock Thayer: A New Biographical Sketch," *The Beethoven Journal* 17/1 (Summer 2002), 2–11 (hereafter cited as Cook, 2002). For a broad portrait of Thayer, especially his last years as American consul in Trieste, see Luigi Bellofatto, *Alex-ander Wheelock Thayer: The Greatest Biographer of Ludwig van Beethoven* (Lewiston, NY: Edwin Mellen Press, 2010).

Beginning in mid-century, Thayer went to Germany to locate as many primary Beethoven documents as he could find, including the composer's letters, the conversation books, and as many of the sketchbooks as were then available. To this he added energetic efforts to find and interview surviving witnesses who had known Beethoven, as well as prominent musicians who could enlarge his perspective. To accomplish these tasks he had to gain the respect of the German musical and literary establishment and then to commit himself to spending most of his later life in Europe so as to remain close to his subject.

Thayer was born in South Natick, Massachusetts, in 1817. He attended Phillips Academy and then Harvard College (A.B., 1843), where he was active in musical circles. He spent several years assisting the Head Librarian at Harvard and began a study of Protestant hymnody, intending to publish an anthology of New England Psalms from 1620 to 1800, a project that never materialized. He took an M.A. in 1846 and an LL.B at Harvard Law School in 1848. Thayer was not highly trained in music, but he had enough musical background to feel at home as the potential biographer of such a major composer, and as his work developed he concentrated on creating a close factual narrative, not on critical or formal discussion of Beethoven's music.

As Thayer came of age Beethoven was becoming the reigning figure in American musical circles, and conspicuously so in Boston. To some degree the cult of Beethoven was the leading edge of the widening domain of serious music, especially in New York and Boston. Admiration for Beethoven came easily to the proponents of the Transcendentalist movement, which had taken root in the intellectual circles around Emerson. American writers and artists caught up in this wave of social and cultural idealism felt that they could inherit and assimilate German philosophy and literature, above all Kant, Goethe, and Schiller, deriving knowledge of them partly through intermediaries such as

Carlyle.[34] Among Thayer's lifetime friends was John Sullivan
Dwight (1813–93), the founder of *Dwight's Journal of Music*,
which ran from 1852 to 1881. This was a serious journal for
music, the first ever in the United States, and Thayer continued to contribute to it for many years, often signing his
articles "The Diarist." Dwight had been at Harvard a decade
earlier than Thayer and he combined what Ora Frishberg
Saloman calls his "musical curiosity and linguistic fluency"
with a belief in the ethical power of music, an idealistic faith
that exposure to great music could improve individuals and
society as a whole.[35] Among Dwight's friends was George
Ripley, the founder of Brook Farm (1841–47), the famous
Utopian community near Boston. Dwight himself was an
original Brook Farm member along with other idealists,
including Margaret Fuller, the writer and editor whose
admiration of Beethoven was such that she wrote a fervent
letter of love and admiration to him in 1843, sixteen years
after the composer's death.[36] The young Thayer flourished
in these circles, and in later years Dwight published several
hundred essays and *feuilletons* sent to him by Thayer. He

[34] For a useful survey of American Transcendentalism in this period as it applies to music see Ora Frishberg Saloman, *Beethoven's Symphonies and J. S. Dwight* (Boston: Northeastern University Press, 1995), Chapters 1 and 2, and sources cited on pp.
181–3.

[35] Saloman's book is a salient contribution to Dwight's background and lifetime contributions, as well as on the significance of the Beethoven symphonies in American cultural life
in the earlier 19 century, especially in Boston and New York.

[36] For Fuller's letter see http://gregmitchellwriter.blogspot.
com/2014/04/a-fuller-love-for-beethoven.html. On Fuller's
love for Beethoven in the context of her time see Charles Cap-
per, *Margaret Fuller: An American Romantic Life, The Public
Years* (Oxford: Oxford University Press, 2005), 57f.

also went to Germany in 1860 and spent some time there with Thayer.[37]

In 1840 and 1841, while still a student, the young Thayer's passion for Beethoven inevitably led him to Schindler's biography (first of all in the Moscheles translation) and to Wegeler-Ries, and when he found errors or discrepancies between them in dates and facts he began assiduous work to straighten them out. As early as 1845 he thought of making a revised edition of Schindler but saw that new research would be needed to give the project weight and substance. In 1849 Thayer sailed to Europe for the first time, settling first in Bonn, "studying German and collecting facts on Beethoven," as he wrote in a later letter.[38]

From then on his course was set. He tried to support himself by writing for *Dwight's Journal* but did not yet have a firm financial footing, and in 1851 he returned to America and went to work for the *New York Tribune*. It was then that headaches arose that were to plague him to the end of his life. Returning to Germany in 1854, he continued his research, traveling and working, meeting many musicians and other people of interest, and in 1865 he secured a lifetime post as United States Consul in Trieste, which he held until his retirement from the diplomatic corps in 1882. He lived on in Trieste until his death in 1897.

Thayer's relentless quest gave him a grasp of Beethoven's biography that was unrivaled in his time. A significant turning point, not always sufficiently appreciated in the literature about him, was his decision to compile a chronological catalogue of Beethoven's works, which he published in Berlin in 1865. This was the third attempt ever to create such a catalogue, as Breitkopf & Härtel had brought one out

---

[37] See Cook 2002, 8.

[38] See TF, vii, for the full text of Thayer's letter to Deiters of August 1, 1878, recounting the basic facts about his earlier life in some detail.

in 1851 and Wilhelm von Lenz had attempted an extensive list in 1854. But Thayer's was a more substantial effort, as he aimed to set up a solid chronology of Beethoven's works, find dates for a large number of minor and lesser known and unpublished works, and provide a basic portrait of the major phases of Beethoven's artistic output.[39] In the preface to this *Chronologisches Verzeichnis* Thayer expressed his hopes for this volume, and his entries for individual compositions include factual details that were then new to most readers.

In a letter of 1878 he wrote with some pride that "I was the first person ever to use Beethoven's Sketch Books for chronology as well as the first to seek out old advertisements and the like."[40] His reference to the sketchbooks, some of which he could consult in Berlin, immediately evokes the name of Gustav Nottebohm, his exact contemporary.[41] It is noteworthy that Thayer was able to get "friendly help" from Nottebohm for his chronological catalogue, as he declares in the preface, especially in view of Nottebohm's reputation as an irascible and demanding personality.[42] He also received significant help from Otto Jahn, a seasoned scholar who was also the first major biographer of Mozart. Jahn generously gave Thayer material that he had been compiling with a view to writing his own Beethoven biography.

---

[39] For a useful account of the *Chronologisches Verzeichnis*, see Bel-lofatto, *Thayer*, 201–09. Thayer's listing included valuable com-ments but did not proceed by using Beethoven's opus numbers for his published works, a method rectified by Nottebohm in his catalogue of 1868 and which remained the standard for later catalogues.

[40] TF, viii.

[41] For a brief account of Nottebohm's accomplishments see my "Nottebohm Revisited," in John Grubbs, ed., *Current Thought in Musicology* (Austin: University of Texas Press,1976), 139–92.

[42] See *Ibid.* for some of the many anecdotes about Nottebohm, his personal characteristics, and his friendship with Brahms.

These years, the early 1860s, also witnessed the first
attempt to publish a complete edition of Beethoven's works
in score, by Breitkopf & Härtel, a project in which Nottebohm was much involved. Astonishing as it may seem in
our time, this project of 1862–65, set up in twenty-four
categories and intended to include all of Beethoven's
completed instrumental and vocal works, remains a fundamental edition of his works that has been reprinted many
times. The Breitkopf complete edition, with its supplement
of 1888 and addenda published still later, is not only still in
circulation but is still, even now, the only one that can as
yet can make any claim to completeness. All this despite its
inevitable shortcomings when compared to the best recent
editions, which benefit from modern textual scholarship.[43]
The replacement for the Breitkopf edition, the modern
series entitled *Beethoven Werke*, edited by scholars under
the auspices of the Beethoven-Haus in Bonn since the early
1950s and published by Henle Verlag, has made great progress over the years – but it is still far from complete. We
must also acknowledge the ongoing work of the intrepid
Beethoven scholar and editor, Jonathan Del Mar, who has
single-handedly edited all the symphonies, with critical
notes, as well as many other works.

In 1868, just three years after Thayer's chronological
catalogue, Nottebohm published his own catalogue of
all of Beethoven's published work. It was a magisterial
achievement for the time, and it laid a foundation for later
catalogues, including that of Kinsky and Halm (1955) and the
recent catalogue by Kurt Dorfmüller, Norbert Gertsch, and

---

[43] In 1957 the Beethoven scholar Willy Hess published his catalogue of "the works by Beethoven not included in the *Gesamtausgabe*" and brought out a series of hitherto unpublished
works.

Julia Ronge (2014), which is now the basic reference book for our time.[44]

But if we consider the state of knowledge in the 1860s, when Beethoven scholarship barely existed, Thayer's attempt to fix a chronology of the works, with additional commentary, was doubly courageous. It shows him seeking to enrich the biographical narrative by first making a close survey of the vast array of Beethoven's compositions, instrumental and vocal, that were the *raison d'être* for the entire enterprise. Inevitably Thayer's *Chronologisches Verzeichnis* was superseded by later and more comprehensive catalogues, but nothing like it was attempted by any of the later 19th-century writers who entered the field of Beethoven biography as a literary and cultural territory, few of whom had anything like Thayer's intellectual tenacity and sense of purpose.

Thayer's biography, taken as a whole in its various languages and versions, is a model of close factual historical research. In many ways it is a product of its time. As he wrote, "I fight for no theories and cherish no prejudices: my sole point of view is the truth." Whatever skepticism this viewpoint may arouse in post-modern minds, Thayer remains the anchor of Beethoven biography. His basic method is to follow the composer's life, year by year, step by step, from

[44] Nottebohm's 1868 catalogue was reprinted as *Thematisches Verzeichnis der im Druck erschienenen Werke von Ludwig van Beethoven*. (Leipzig: Breitkopf & Härtel, 1925). Kinsky-Halm's massive catalogue was published with the title *Das Werk Beethovens; Thematisch-Bibliographisches Verzeichnis seiner sämtlichen vollendeten Kompositionen* (Munich: G. Henle Verlag, 1955); and the new catalogue, edited by Kurt Dorfmüller, Norbert Gertsch, and Julia Ronge bears the title *Ludwig van Beethoven: Thematisch-bibliographisches Werkverzeichnis*, 2 vols. (Munich: G. Henle, 2014). Volume 1, 41*–46* provides (in English) a detailed history of the various Beethoven thematic catalogues from 1851 to 2014.

his boyhood in Bonn to his later years in Vienna, including as much context as possible. His relentlessly chronological approach may seem old-fashioned in modern times, as do some of his judgments about Beethoven's sometimes aberrant behavior – but its solidity is beyond question. Thayer's purpose was to establish as true a historical narrative as could be made from the facts, and he was the first ever to do so.

We can see his critical side in his reviews of other books on Beethoven that had appeared in his lifetime, among them his review of A. B. Marx's *Beethoven: Leben und Schaffen* of 1859, in *The Atlantic Monthly* in 1860.[45] Despite Marx's well-established reputation as a music critic and theorist, Thayer excoriated his account of Beethoven's life as "a thing manufactured to sell," "a disgrace to the institution in which its author occupies the station of Professor." [46]

In Thayer's time there was no such thing as a field of musicology. There were book-length music histories in German, like those of Kiesewetter and Ambros, there were biographies like those of Winterfeld on Gabrieli, Jahn on Mozart, and Spitta on Bach – and there were the first attempts at critical editions of the music of major composers, above all the Bach-Gesellschaft edition and the Breitkopf edition of Beethoven's *Werke*. But there was no professional society or organization of musicologists yet in existence, no sense of contribution to a well-populated field of studies. Thayer's work was directed to music-lovers, to Beethoven admirers, and to the world.

---

[45] Theodore Albrecht, "Thayer contra Marx: A Warning from 1860; An Edited Reprint of Thayer's Review of Marx's Beethoven Biography," *Beethoven Journal* 14/1 (Summer 1999), 2–8; and 14/2 (Winter 1999), 56–64. Thayer's pungent prose, slightly edited by Albrecht, speaks to his uncompromising view of his chosen field of studies better than any description.

[46] *Ibid.*, 14/2, 61, col. 2.

The intellectual context for Thayer includes the role of history as a grand discipline in the hands of the German historians of the 19th century, led by Leopold von Ranke (1795–1886). Ranke's aim was to uncover historical truth about the periods and subjects he explored, to write the history of earlier times "as it actually had been" [*wie es eigentlich gewesen*], the catchphrase that became the watchword of historical positivism. Scholarship meant separating myth from fact, along with the need to interpret the facts and develop them into convincing narratives that reflect not only what the documents tell us happened, but also strive to interpret the thought behind the historical artifact.

Thayer's status as an American working in a major field of European music, above all on the dominating figure of Beethoven, also deserves comment. He belonged to the generation of American and especially New England historians who were making important contributions to European history. His contemporaries included the venerated William Prescott (1796–1859), the master historian of Spain and of the Spanish conquests of Mexico and Peru; and John Lothrop Motley (1814–77) whose history of the Netherlands was a major achievement.[47] Motley, like Thayer, spent years in Europe in the American diplomatic service, first in Saint Petersburg and then in Vienna, from 1861 to 1867, where in fact Thayer served as his "Secretary of the Legation."[48] It is also of interest that all three had been trained at Harvard, then a center of interest in European history and culture.

---

[47] For discussion of Prescott and Motley in the context of American historians of the early 19th century see G. P. Gooch, *History and Historians in the Nineteenth Century*, 3rd edition (London: Longmans, Green and Co., 1920), Chapter XXI ("The United States").

[48] I am indebted here, as elsewhere in my discussion of Thayer, to Grant Cook, who has specialized in the study of Thayer's biography.

Since Thayer made it his business to get to know as many musicians and Beethoven enthusiasts as possible, he inevitably sought out Schindler, and he actually met him twice during his travels in Germany. They first met in October 1854, in Frankfurt. Observations by Thayer survive from this encounter, and in one of them he describes Schindler as "a tall man, face somewhat marked with a small pox, very erect in his carriage, and near upon his 60th year."[49] Among other subjects they spoke of Beethoven's relationship to his brothers Carl and Johann – but we do not have a more detailed record of their conversation.

In 1860 he went to see Schindler again, now in the town of Bockenheim near Frankfurt. This meeting took place just as the third and last edition of Schindler's biography had appeared. And now we find Thayer displaying generous personal sympathy for Schindler in describing their meeting. In his account for *Dwight's Journal*, Thayer writes:

> ...for more than twenty years he [Schindler] has been one of the 'best abused' men in Germany. In how far he has deserved the treatment which he has received from Spohr, Mendelssohn, Dorn, and from the partisans of each in the German musical world, it is not our purpose to inquire... Musicians in all parts of Germany will warn you against Schindler, as being unworthy of credence – and, yet however writers upon Beethoven plunder him![50]

He goes on to say that Schindler,

> however much mistaken in many minor points in his book, owing to insufficient data, and to errors of correspondents, is a perfectly honest writer, and fired with a love and veneration for Beethoven's memory, which seems to increase with advancing age...[51]

---

[49] Bellofatto, *Thayer*, 69; and Cook 2002, 3.

[50] *The Musical World*, January 7, 1860, 12–13, containing Thayer's review of Schindler entitled "Schindler's Life of Beethoven."

[51] Cook 2002, 8.

We now realize that Thayer could know nothing about Schindler's forgeries in the conversation books, which he would have despised, and by 1860 he was more aware than anyone of Schindler's mistakes about dates and events. In Thayer's review of Schindler's third edition he fills two dense columns of prose with corrections of factual errors. Accordingly, we can't help being struck by his benevolent description of the man, whose carelessness and self-promotion stood opposed to all that Thayer believed in. Here was Thayer, encountering the man who had produced what was accepted as the major Beethoven biography of the age, despite all its problems – while Thayer himself had been devoting his mortal energy to constructing an accurate and responsible portrait of the same man. Yet Thayer writes of Schindler, after this second meeting, with empathy and kindness. Perhaps there was one aspect of Schindler and his experience that, for Thayer, might have compensated for Schindler's lack of intellectual discipline – that there had been a time in his earlier life when Schindler had been right there in the room with Beethoven, had been an eye-witness, a member of the inner circle. Perhaps Thayer could feel that now in 1860, face to face with Schindler, what he was hearing was personal testimony, based not on documents or on second-hand reports, but on the one experience that Thayer could never have – that is, Schindler's memories of Beethoven's tone of voice, his physical presence, his gestures in conversation – in all, his direct contact with the living Beethoven.

Lenz, Marx, and Nohl

We come now to three writers on Beethoven of the early and mid-19th century whose writings are only partly biographical but whose comments on his music are still occasionally cited by modern authors: Wilhelm von Lenz, Adolph Bernhard Marx, and Ludwig Nohl. They are admittedly secondary figures in my survey of biographers and commentators, but their accomplishments still have some importance in our time. Of the three, Marx in particular still holds his place in the history of music theory for his contributions on musical form and related subjects in vocal and instrumental music, from Gluck to Beethoven. Lenz on the other hand is remembered essentially for his publications on Beethoven. Ludwig Nohl, writing some years later, spread his talents more widely than the other two and was much more a popularizer than they, but nevertheless his publications still have some value in modern Beethoven scholarship.

Wilhelm von Lenz

Wilhelm von Lenz (1809–83) was a Russian musician of German descent who studied piano in Paris with Liszt in the late 1820s and with Moscheles in London. In later life he held a position as a state official in St Petersburg. Lenz produced two critical books on Beethoven that remained in circulation for many years – his *Beethoven et ses trois styles* (1852) and his *Beethoven: Eine Kunst-Studie* (1855). In 1860 he brought out a "Critical Catalogue of the Complete Works of Ludwig van Beethoven" that was not on the same level as Thayer's catalogue of 1865 nor, certainly, Nottebohm's of 1868.

Lenz's first book, mainly centered on the piano sonatas, is often associated with the three-period division of Beethoven's lifetime achievements. In fact the idea had been proposed as early as 1818 by a French writer and again in 1828 by Schlosser in his feeble biography – but with Lenz it became the commonplace in Beethoven commentary that it still remains, despite objections by more than one modern author, including Joseph Kerman.[52] Lenz's second book,

---

[52] Joseph Kerman and Alan Tyson, *The New Grove Beethoven* (New York: W. W. Norton & Co., 1980 and 1993), 89–94; "The "three periods" For further discussions see James Webster, "The Concept of Beethoven's Early Period in the Context of

Beethoven: Eine Kunst-Studie is a large-scale overview of Beethoven's entire output and is still worth examining. Lenz often quotes earlier commentators throughout, which makes his *Kunst-Studie* a potentially useful rough guide to much of the earlier literature, though I know of no later Beethoven study that has sifted through the book from this viewpoint.

Beethoven et ses trois styles sprang to life as a critique of a recent Mozart biography by Alexander Oulibicheff, a fellow Russian, who in turn retaliated with a polemic of 1857 entitled *Beethoven, ses Critiques et ses Glossateurs.*[53] For Oulibicheff, a Mozart devotee, Beethoven's mature works were thorny and difficult, and his last works were decadent and incomprehensible. This viewpoint was not as extreme as we might think, in our time, and in fact it persisted through the later 19th century in many musical circles, gradually changing only in the 20th century.[54] As to the reception of Lenz's work by German contemporaries who regarded Beethoven as their own cultural property, he had some correspondence with Schindler, on whose 1840 biography he had drawn for some of his material.[55] This did not prevent or mitigate Schindler's negative remarks on Lenz, as well as on others who had entered the competition.[56]

Periodizations in General," *BF* 3 (1994), 1–29; and Glenn Stanley, "Some Thoughts on biography and a chronology of Beethoven's life and music," in *the Cambridge Companion to Beethoven* (Cambridge: Cambridge University Press, 2000), 3–13.

[53] On Lenz, Oulibicheff and their conflict see Brenner, *Schindler*, 122ff and especially 125–29.

[54] For a critique of the changing interpretations of Beethoven's last period see Kristin Knittel, *From Chaos to History: the Reception of Beethoven's Late Quartets* (Princeton University Diss., 1992 (UMI No. 9230234)).

[55] See Brenner, *Schindler,* 121–29 and for the correspondence, 431–69.

[56] See *Ibid.,* 130 for a letter from Schindler of 1858 on Lenz, Marx, and Oulibicheff.

Adolph Bernhard Marx

Adolph Bernard Marx (1795–1866) was the first editor of the
Berliner Allgemeine Musikalische Zeitung, founded in 1824
by the publisher Adolph Martin Schlesinger. Within a year
Marx wrote laudatory reviews of no fewer than eight works
by Beethoven, which brought him favorable acknowledg-
ment from the composer in two letters to Schlesinger (of 19
July 1825 and again on 31 May 1826).[57]

As music theorist Marx made his name with his trea-
tise on composition (1837), and in 1859 he followed with his
Beethoven biography, *Ludwig van Beethoven: Leben und
Schaffen*. He is deservedly remembered for his pedagogical
innovations and for his early recognition of sonata form as
a governing principle, from Haydn to his own time. But it
was his Beethoven *Life and Work* that made his public reputation, and it went through many later editions. It is much
more valuable for Marx's comments on the works than for
his account of Beethoven's life, for which, as we saw, he was
castigated by Thayer in a trenchant review. What remains
significant is that it was the first major Beethoven biography to be written by a musical intellectual whose primary
orientation was not music history or biography, but rather
formal analysis, and in recent writings, especially by Scott
Burnham, Marx's work has received deserved recognition.[58]

Ludwig Nohl

Ludwig Nohl (1831–85), more than a generation younger
than Marx, came to music after an early preparation in law
and became a noted biographer of several major musicians.
Beginning in the early 1860s Nohl turned out biographies of
Mozart (1863), Beethoven (1864), Haydn (1880), and Liszt

---

[57] *Briefwechsel* Nos. 2147 and 2157.
[58] Scott Burnham, *Beethoven Hero* (Princeton; Princeton University Press, 1995).

(1882), plus other books on musical subjects. He worked on a broad canvas, and by including letters and other documents alongside discussion of music, his work continued to have interest for later scholars.[59]

Nohl's reach included, for example, his being the first to publish the autograph manuscript of Beethoven's famous little piano piece, "Für Elise" (WoO 59), which had been unknown when he brought it out in 1867.[60] Much more important was his work on Beethoven's *Tagebuch* of 1812–18, a valuable document of Beethoven's inner thoughts during these difficult years. Though Nohl could not locate the original manuscript of the *Tagebuch*, which in fact has never been found, he got hold of one of the extant copies and published a version of the text. About this Solomon writes, "he is to be credited for identifying many of the quotations and literary extracts" that the diary contains, "although his annotations in other respects are unreliable and fragmentary."[61] Despite Solomon's carefully annotated publication of it, the *Tagebuch* tends to remain overshadowed, among Beethoven documents, by the Heiligenstadt Testament of 1802 and the "Immortal Beloved" letter of 1812. Yet many

---

[59] See W. Barclay Squire and M. Musgrave, article "Nohl" in Grove Music Online. For Maynard Solomon's remarks, see the excellent "Selected Bibliography" that ends his *Beethoven*, 2nd rev. edn (1998), 496 (on Nohl's publication of the diary of Fanny Giannatasio) and 497, where his *Beethovens Leben* 3 vols., (Leipzig: Günther, 1864) is called "a pathbreaking work utilizing original sources and interviews."

[60] Nohl's publication of *Für Elise* appeared in his edition of *Neue Briefe Beethovens* (Stuttgart: J. G. Cotta, 1867), 28–33; see LvB-WV, Vol. 2, 145ff.

[61] Solomon, "Beethoven's Tagebuch of 1812–1818," in A. Tyson, ed., *Beethoven Studies* 3 (Cambridge: Cambridge University Press, 1982), 203.

of the entries in this diary are deeply revealing, embodying Beethoven's innermost reflections, his outlook on his personal difficulties, his deafness, and his resolve to maintain his productivity – all this in the years after 1812 in which he was moving gradually but decisively from the heroic style of his middle years into the new world of his last period.

Although Nohl's work shows his wide range of interests and his pursuit of sources, it largely remains in the shadows. As Theodore Albrecht notes in his edition of letters to Beethoven, Nohl was the first to attempt a collection of Beethoven letters, and his work deserves mention despite Thayer's criticism. Nohl promoted his volume of slightly more than four hundred letters as "the first complete edition of Beethoven's letters" but Thayer pointed out that in his own private collection there were more than three hundred letters that were not known to Nohl, and that of seventy letters published by Nohl that were new to Thayer, most of them came from "the papers of the recently deceased Schindler." He also complained that many of the letters were given by Nohl only in "short extracts."[62] German critics were no less severe. A review of Nohl's volume of letters in the *Leipzig Grenzboten Journal* was even harsher than Thayer, as we see from this excerpt:

> ...all the carelessness which characterized him in the biography of Beethoven, come before us in this collection of letters. If Professor Nohl goes on making books in this superficial manner, he may perhaps impose on children and the ignorant, but the higher criticism will not be able to take further notice of him.[63]

[62] Bellofatto, *Thayer*, 254, quoting a letter written by Thayer in 1865 and published in Stuttgart in that year, then quoted in *Dwight's Journal of Music* of 18 August 1866.

[63] *Ibid.*, 255, a commentary from the Leipzig *Grenzboten* journal of March 1866, which was published in translation in *Dwight's Journal of Music*, July 4 and 18, 1868.

Nottebohm on the Composer at Work

The third significant figure in Beethoven commentary in these years was Gustav Nottebohm. Now Nottebohm's reputation is based on his studies of the Beethoven sketchbooks, along with his other essays focused on Beethoven as composer, not on his personal life or social and political context.

But Nottebohm's pathbreaking research on Beethoven's creative life – the composer's inner world – secures him a major place in any study of the Beethoven literature and helps to broaden and deepen our concept of biography. More than a few of his essays deal with subjects other than sketches. They concern aspects of individual works in themselves, such as "The Excluded Two Bars in the Third Movement of the C Minor Symphony" (N I, VI) or "The Bagatelles Op. 119." (N II, XVIII); or topics such as "Metronome Markings" (N I, XXVI).[64] Equally important was his extended study of Beethoven's studies with Haydn, Albrechtsberger, and Salieri, which came out as a separate book in 1873.[65]

The bulk of Nottebohm's published work shows that he was conversant with Beethoven's life and career in broader and human terms, as the index to his *Beethoveniana* and *Zweite Beethoveniana* makes clear.

In fact my inclusion of Nottebohm among the "biographers," in the broadest sense, stems from his own words, as

---

[64] Nottebohm's first collection of essays, his *Beethoveniana* appeared in 1872; his second and more substantial collection, the *Zweite Beethoveniana*, came out in 1887, after his death, edited by Eusebius Mandycewski; for full details see the Bibliography, N I and N II.

[65] Nottebohm first discussed and corrected earlier scholarship on this material in his *Beethoveniana* (1872) Essay XXIX; and in 1873 published his own study of the material in his *Beethovens Studien* (1873). The recent book by Julia Ronge, *Beethovens Lehrzeit*, breaks new ground in this territory.

cited by his editor, Eusebius Mandycewski, in the introduction to Nottebohm's most important volume of essays, the *Zweite Beethoveniana* of 1887. This volume was published five years after Nottebohm's death, though most of its contents had previously appeared in periodicals during his lifetime.[66] Mandycewski provides a brief foreword, signed by himself, in which he says that "The Introduction [which then follows and is unsigned] had to be put together from various available indications," which must mean that he is drawing upon Nottebohm's posthumous papers. The "Introduction" begins as follows:

> What is the aim of these essays? To put it briefly, they are (except for some of them, which pursue other aims) biographical contributions, in the sense that the word 'biographical' is meant to refer to the working artist, and 'contributions' refers almost exclusively to studies of Beethoven's working papers and sketch leaves[67]

"The word 'biographical' is meant to refer to the working artist..." With these words Nottebohm establishes an alternative view of what an artist's biography can be about – that if well-established evidence exists, a biography can probe the artist's inner world. Implicit in his stress on the word "biographisch" (and it is given with quotation marks) is that he is not dealing mainly, maybe not even partially, with the normal stuff of biography – a narrative of the living person in his complex interactions with the world around him, his personal evolution. This claim may well imply a critique of the purely factual biographies of Beethoven that were

---

[66] See my "Nottebohm Revisited," 139–92.

[67] N II "Einleitung," vii: "*Was diese Aufsätze sollen? Um es kurz zu sagen, es sollen (mit Ausnahme einiger, die ein anderes Ziel verfolgen) biographische Beiträge sein, das Wort 'biographisch' nur auf den schaffenden Künstler bezogen, und 'Beiträge' beinahe ausschliesslich aus Arbeitsbüchern und Skizzenblättern Beethoven's geschöpft.*"

coming out in his time, certainly that of Schindler, many of whose mistakes Nottebohm corrects in footnotes in his essays.[68] As for Thayer and his intense labors on the factual dimensions of Beethoven's life, which Nottebohm in his sterner moods would have seen as external to his principal concerns, we have good reason to believe that he respected Thayer's work. We saw earlier that Nottebohm gave Thayer material help when he was compiling his thematic catalogue in the early 1860s, and we know from Hermann Deiters, Thayer's translator, that Nottebohm carefully annotated Thayer's thematic catalogue of 1865 and that Deiters was able to incorporate many of Nottebohm's annotations into his translation.

The two kinds of inquiry, that of Nottebohm and that of Thayer, are like pathways on two sides of a mountain, and their authors are like mountaineers who climb it from opposite sides. This difference frames a basic issue in artistic biography – that is, the biographer can choose between a main focus on the artist as a person in the world, or on the works as products of the thought and feeling, the artistic vision by which the artist produced them. This second approach, which in Beethoven's case is greatly facilitated by the survival of the large mass of sketchbooks and related sources, tends to see the works as the necessity that shapes the life, a life that is centrally devoted to bringing the works into the world. That must be the sense in which Nottebohm could see himself as a biographer. At the same time Nottebohm's

[68] The detailed index to N I and N II was made by Mandycewski and published in 1888 as an appendix to N II, with a brief introduction. It is included at the end of the 1970 reprint of N II (New York; Johnson Reprint Corporation). Under "Schindler" in the index are numerous entries in which Nottebohm commented on, and/or corrected, Schindler.

essays show many references to Thayer, sometimes acknowledging a factual point, sometimes correcting one.[69]

More than Schindler or Thayer, Nottebohm was a highly trained musician, a pianist, theorist, and composer whose seriousness of purpose and background brought him into close contact with Johannes Brahms, who remained one of Nottebohm's admirers throughout his life.[70] After studying piano in Berlin with Ludwig Berger and composition with Siegfried Dehn, Nottebohm went to Leipzig in the early 1840s, where he studied at the Conservatory. His teachers included Robert Schumann, with whom he had correspondence, and Felix Mendelssohn, who wrote him a testimonial letter in 1843.[71]

Nottebohm then moved to Vienna in 1846, where he settled for good, and it was there that he met Brahms in the 1860s. As Brahms wrote in a letter to the publisher Rieter-Biedermann in 1870:

> I am no scholar, and I should not attach my recommendation to Nottebohm's work... But you may be certain that it is the result of immense industry and will be of the highest interest to artists, connoisseurs, and amateurs."[72]

Brahms recommended theory pupils to Nottebohm, who also stood out among other members of Brahms's

---

[69] The index to N II shows 29 references to Thayer's writings in Nottebohm's two volumes, and distinguishes between those in which he is "mentioned" and those in which he is "corrected."

[70] For summaries of his career see my "Nottebohm Revisited," and Douglas Johnson, article "Nottebohm" in *The New Grove Dictionary of Music and Musicians*, ed. Stanley Sadie, 1st edn (London: Macmillan), Vol. 13, 429–30.

[71] On the faculty at Leipzig in the 1840s see R. Larry Todd, *Mendelssohn: A Life in Music* (Oxford: Oxford University Press, 2003), 451 and, on the letter from Mendelssohn, 617, n. 25.

[72] Quoted in Hans Joachim Moser, "Westfälische Lebensbilder," (Münster: LWL, 1957), 140 (for the full citation see my "Nottebohm Revisited," 186, notes 2 and 3.

circle because Nottebohm, a thorny and demanding personality, was a fellow North German. His study of the
Beethoven sketchbooks must have been deeply mean-
ingful to Brahms, who had a strong interest in history
and whose instrumental works, in all their originality and
power, preserved the basic genres and formal structures
that Beethoven had bequeathed.

The power of Beethoven's legacy is nowhere more visible
in the later 19th century than in the opposed aesthetic viewpoints of Brahms and Wagner. Though they developed in
entirely different ways, both saw Beethoven as their guiding
star. And in this period of late Romanticism, with the continued expansion of concert life in which the orchestral and
chamber works of Beethoven were now established classics,
biographies were now being written for the bookshelves of
every musician and music-lover. By about 1900 the writings
of Schindler and Thayer – and in specialized musical circles,
those of Nottebohm – stood as monuments of biographical
achievement, but other biographies were becoming available
and not only in German. As the idea of a field of musicology
began to grow in intellectual circles, first in Germany and
then in the English-speaking world, the book-length surveys
of his life and works stood as both summations of what was
known and as challenges to new research that might yield
new perspectives.

Richard Wagner and G. E. Anders: A Projected
Beethoven Biography (1841)

As unexpected as it may be to find Richard Wagner included
among Beethoven biographers, at least as a matter of
intention, evidence shows that in his early years the young
Wagner seriously thought of collaborating on a biography
of the composer who was already his godlike artistic model.
Born in 1813, Wagner's teenage years coincided with Beethoven's last period. Though his primary musical influences

were in German romantic opera, including Weber's *Der Freischütz*, they also included Beethoven's Ninth Symphony. Wagner studied the Ninth with close attention and arranged the whole gigantic work for piano in 1830–31.[73] Thereafter, knowing, conducting, and writing about the Ninth Symphony became a lifetime passion, and it remained a fundamental element in his artistic imagination from beginning to end.[74] This was never better symbolized than with his performance of the Ninth at the ceremony for laying the foundation of the *Festspielhaus* at Bayreuth in 1872.[75]

As early as 1840 Wagner wrote his fictional novella, *A Pilgrimage to Beethoven,* in which he prefigures his conviction that the new music drama he would eventually create had its roots in Beethoven's decision to add voices to the symphony in the Ninth. And Beethoven remains a major figure in many of his later essays, including *Oper und Drama* (1861). His culminating tribute to Beethoven was his essay of 1870 for the Beethoven centenary, simply entitled *Beethoven.* By then Wagner's adoration of Beethoven was suffused with the nationalism that was sweeping Germany in this year of military victory and political unification after the Franco-Prussian war. It is also one of the strongest

---

[73] For a sample page see *The Wagner Compendium*, ed. Barry Millington (London: Thames and Hudson, 1992), Plate 21, facing 208.

[74] Recent studies of this topic include Klaus Kropfinger, *Wagner und Beethoven* (Regensburg: Gustav Bosse Verlag, 1975), also available in English as *Wagner and Beethoven: Richard Wagner's Reception of Beethoven,* trans. Peter Palmer (Cambridge: Cambridge University Press, 1991) but with the caveat that the English translation does not include the full documentation found in the German version. Another important recent contribution is Christopher Reynolds, *Wagner, Schumann, and the Lessons of Beethoven's Ninth* (Berkeley: University of California Press, 2015).

[75] Millington, *The Wagner Compendium,* 101.

statements of Wagner's later aesthetic views as they were mediated through the philosophy of Schopenhauer.[76]

The idea of a Beethoven biography came up in the years 1839–41, when the young Wagner, then in his late twenties, was trying to make his way as an opera composer in Paris, then the cultural capital of western Europe. At this time his small circle of acquaintances included a certain Gottfried Engelbert Anders, originally from Bonn, who was employed as a librarian at the Paris Conservatoire. Anders, a somewhat mysterious individual, was a Beethoven enthusiast of a high order. Wagner reports in *Mein Leben* that Anders was not his real name, but Wagner does not say and perhaps did not know what his real name was.[77] Evidently Anders had assembled a mass of information about Beethoven with a view to writing a biography and, in 1839, the year of Wagner's arrival in Paris, Anders published a French translation of the *Biographische Notizen* by Wegeler and Ries, just one year after its appearance in German.[78]

Two years later, in 1841, Anton Schindler came to Paris, to flaunt his role as the first and supposedly most authoritative of Beethoven biographers, presenting himself as an eye witness to Beethoven and hoping to expand his reputation.[79] It was then that Heinrich Heine voiced his classic description of Schindler as the self-styled "Ami de Beethoven."[80] In

---

[76] See the recent translation by Roger Allen, *Richard Wagner's Beethoven (1870)* (Woodbridge: The Boydell Press, 2014), with its extended and informative introduction.

[77] In Millington, *The Wagner Compendium*, 22, the entry for "Anders, Gottfried" says that he was "of aristocratic lineage" and that "his original surname was Bettendorf (or Bethendorf)."

[78] As given by Leo Schrade in his *Beethoven in France* (New Haven: Yale University Press, 1942), 259, n. 3, the title was *Details biographiques sur Beethoven d'après Wegeler et Ries* (Paris: Revue et Gazette Musicale, 1839).

[79] On Schindler in Paris see Brenner, *Schindler*, 84ff.

[80] Frequently quoted, my citation is from Brenner, *Schindler*, 84.

typical style, Schindler denounced Anders's translation of
Wegeler-Ries, an action that actually led to a meeting called
by the publisher, Maurice Schlesinger, with Anders and
Wagner both present, at which Anders vehemently denied
Schindler's claim that he had altered Wegeler and Ries's text
in any way, whereupon, according to Wagner,

> ...the flashing eyes of Beethoven's liegeman grew moist,
> and... he... assured him that... he solemnly swore to make
> handsome amends in the second edition of his book.[81]

As Klaus Kropfinger points out in his book on Wagner
and Beethoven, Schindler did make amends in 1842 with a
monograph called *Beethoven in Paris*, an account of his own
meetings with important French musicians and Beethoven
enthusiasts, including Berlioz, Chopin, and others, to whom
he showed Beethoven documents and a Beethoven portrait,
claiming that "all salons were open to me..."[82]

Wagner's opinion of Schindler's biography was brisk
and clear: it was "very incomplete, besides being written
incoherently and in a dull and clumsy way."[83] And soon it
became clear that Wagner and Anders were hatching a plan
to work together on a new biography, with Anders providing
the basic factual framework on works and dates, and with
Wagner writing the text with what he declared would be
his characteristic freedom of conception and style. Here is a
telling excerpt from a letter Wagner wrote to Theodor Winkler, an acquaintance in Leipzig at this time.

> Our biography of Beethoven will be a book in two vol-
> umes, each having about 30 sheets of medium-sized

---

[81] Kropfinger, *Wagner und Beethoven*, [English translation un-
less otherwise noted.], 60, quoting Wagner from *Gesammelte
Schriften und Dichtungen*, (Leipzig: Breitkopf & Härtel, 1907),
Vol. xii, 82ff.

[82] Brenner, *Schindler*, 86f. and Kropfinger, *Wagner und Beethoven*, 56ff.

[83] Kropfinger, *Wagner und Beethoven*, 60.

print, containing an accurate and detailed account of both
the great master's artistic and domestic life, written in
persuasive and, to match its subject, perhaps imaginative
terms. Our book will avoid any pedantic display of scholarship, being more a great novel about an artist than a dry
listing of data and anecdotes compiled in chronological
order; but for all that, there will be no statements that
cannot stand up to the most thorough and meticulous
historical scrutiny. At the same time, however, there will
be woven into the historical account a detailed review and
description of the great musical epoch that was produced
by Beethoven's genius and extended from his works to all
the more modern music. Among other things, this biography will include a complete catalogue of Beethoven's
works in chronological order – something we have never
had up to now, together with facsimiles and the like. At
all events it will be the fullest and most detailed work that
anyone could publish about Beethoven.[84]

Much of this is astonishing, above all Wagner's claim that
this book would stand up to "the most thorough and meticulous historical scrutiny," and that it would contain a full
catalogue of Beethoven's works and "facsimiles and the like".
For a moment we might think that we are reading a statement by Thayer (about whom I know of no evidence that
Wagner ever referred to him, though he might have been
aware of Thayer-Deiters's first volume when it came out in
1866). But in this grandiose plan for a Beethoven biography,
the novelist and dramatist in Wagner takes over, with his
ambition to make this projected book "a great novel about
an artist."

It is hardly surprising that Wagner never wrote this or any
biography of Beethoven, as his intense creative ambitions
grew ever greater and led on to his early romantic operas, to

[84] *Ibid.,* 62; the original text is in Wagner's *Sämtliche Briefe, Vol.
I: 1830–42,* ed. Gertrud Strobel and Werner Wolf. (Leipzig:
Deutscher Verlag für Musik, 1967), 483.

Oper und Drama, to his late masterpieces of music drama and his immense artistic legacy. And yet his description of this abortive biography rings with the same dedication to Beethoven's memory that is embedded in his critical writings. As Kropfinger pointed out, Wagner's novella of 1840, *A Pilgrimage to Beethoven,* and his *Beethoven* essay of 1870 partly reflected in different ways this early idea for a comprehensive biography.

As noted above, I have found no references to the work of Thayer in the Wagner literature, though Kropfinger suggests that he might have seen reviews of works by Lenz in 1855 and Oulibicheff in 1857, and that the same periodical that carried the Oulibicheff review later published a review of Thayer's first volume by Ludwig Bischoff in 1866.[85] On the other hand, Nohl (an avowed Wagner disciple) published scathing remarks on both Thayer and Nottebohm in his *Beethoven, Liszt, Wagner* of 1874.[86] The only reference to Nottebohm that I have found in the Wagner literature is in Cosima Wagner's diary entry for 15 May 1875, in which she writes:

> We occupy ourselves with Beethoven's sketches for the 9th Symphony, edited by Nottebohm – very strange how trivial almost, how commonplace the most significant themes when first written down; R[ichard] says it is like that with him – what he first writes down he can hardly ever use just in that way; it is a sort of indication that one has something in mind, quite different, which one then finds again...[87]

---

[85] *Ibid.,* 256, n. 4.

[86] *Ibid.,* 249 (with quotations from Nohl).

[87] *Ibid.,* 61, reference; the quotation is from *Cosima Wagner's Diaries, 1869–1877.* Vol. 1, translated by Geoffrey Skelton, ed by Martin Gregor-Dellin and Dietrich Mack (New York: Harcourt Brace Jovanovich, 1976), 846.

1. Karl Holz: photograph of a miniature portrait by Betty Frölich.

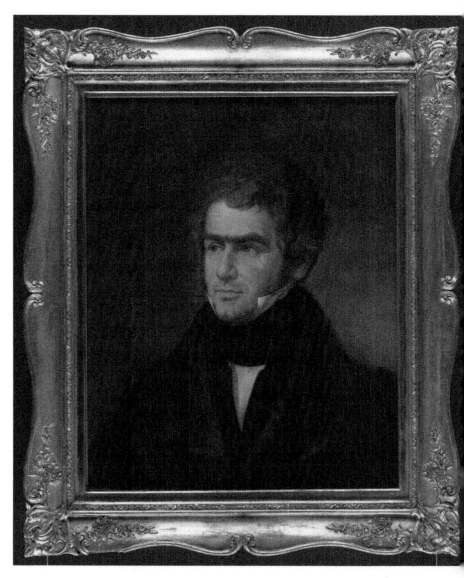

2. Ferdinand Ries portrait: anonymous oil painting.

3. Franz Wegeler portrait: painting by Johann Heinrich Richter.

4. Anton Schindler: reproduction of a photograph.

5. Alexander Wheelock Thayer: photograph by Emil Koch (1890).

6. Ludwig Nohl.

7. Gustav Nottebohm.

8. Theodor Frimmel (1853–1928),
photograph by Alois Beer.

3

The Late Nineteenth and Early Twentieth Centuries

The Newly Enlarged Context for Beethoven Biography

THE BEETHOVEN CENTENARY IN 1870 brought a flood of commentaries, much of it criticism, some of it biography. By then, forty-odd years after his death, his image had been raised to the point of veneration, thanks to continued admiration by composers, performers, conductors, critics, concert audiences, and the general public. The major works of his middle years were by now established classics, while the more rarefied late works, especially the last quartets, were still awaiting broad acceptance. Beethoven the man was seen as the embodiment of the resolute and powerful individual who was resolved to overcome his deafness, and his overcoming now began to dominate the biographical narratives even more than before. "I will seize Fate by the throat," he had written in a famous letter, and those words sank into the minds of those who were now seeking to portray him to the world at large.

In Germany and Europe, this year, 1870, was a major turning point, as the German states came together to form a nation – the German Empire, with Bismarck as its *Reichskanzler*, its imperial chancellor. The new political unity solidified national pride in German cultural achievements, most of all its musical traditions. Certainly German literature, philosophy, and art – Goethe, Kant, Dürer – were greatly admired by the German literate public, but German music – Bach, Mozart, Beethoven – was of world-wide importance. The increasing numbers of performing institutions – above all, symphony orchestras who could perform the Beethoven symphonies in their concert halls – made his image even larger than before.

Among devotees of new music between 1870 and about 1920, his influence was becoming intermingled with that of composers of the mid- and late Romantic periods in Germany and France. By the turn of the century basic principles of musical style and expression were changing more sharply than ever before, as these decades witnessed the erosion and, in some quarters, the rejection of romanticism and the rise of new modes of expression. These included French impressionism, with Debussy and Ravel; the monumental orchestral works of Mahler and Richard Strauss; the intensified *verismo* of Italian opera in Puccini, and much more. These years saw the extension of tonality beyond its traditional frameworks, as progressive composers grappled with a variety of post-tonal approaches to musical structure. The most radical developments would lead in due course from atonality to the twelve-tone language of Schönberg, but the same period also witnessed other powerful innovations in musical thought and expression with Stravinsky, Bartók, and Varèse. And outside the portals of art music, the province of the high bourgeoisie, popular music in all its broad emotional appeal and accessibility was growing in scope and significance for general audiences who found the new trends in art music beyond their horizons of interest and expectation.

Against this larger background, Beethoven was becoming ever more a patriarchal figure of the deeper past, a primary figure-head of the canon that now dominated concert music and was becoming embedded in Western cultural life – as to some degree it still is. A close study of the changing views of Beethoven from the 1920s down to the later twentieth century was made by Hans Heinrich Eggebrecht in his penetrating study of the history of Beethoven reception, first published in 1972 and reissued in an amplified edition in 1994.[1] The special field of Beethoven biography can also be seen against the backdrop of this general cultural situation, this age of "modernity," in all the complex meanings of that term. The enlargement of cultural institutions, including, as Jerrold Seigel puts it, "books and periodicals, museums, and concert venues...," was symptomatic.[2]

For music, its transmission and, in a larger sense, its modes of existence, by far the most important enlargement was the invention of recording, which now promised to transform musical experience. It began with Edison's invention of the "gramophone" in the 1870s – and how vastly this technology developed in later decades, and is still developing in the digital age, needs no underlining. The advent of recorded music was, for listeners and musicians alike, a new way of having music. Now one could passively experience music without having to attend concerts or even play or sing it at home; the eventual change was nothing less than revolutionary. In the broad sweep of history the invention of recording appears to have been as important a turning point for the transmission of music as had been, in earlier epochs, the rise of musical notation in the early middle ages, and the printing of polyphonic music in the Renaissance. And it is surely obvious now, in the 21st century, that the commercial ramifications of this invention have had a

[1] Hans Heinrich Eggebrecht, *Zur Geschichte der Beethoven Rezeption*, (1st edn Mainz: Akademie der Wissenschaften, 1972; 2nd edn Laaber: Laaber-Verlag, 1994).

[2] Jerrold Seigel, *Modernity and Bourgeois Life* (Cambridge: Cambridge University Press, 2012), 414. This book illuminates many of the most important background developments that lie behind the transformation of the Beethoven image, as conveyed through performances of his music, his image, and, as outlined in this book, his biographies.

transforming effect on musical culture, world-wide, and that the commodification of music, on a vast scale, has been consequential for the vast domain of what we now think of, and label, classical music. Accordingly, Beethoven's public stature has grown still further, both in the West and beyond its borders, as the world entered the age of electronic communication, cyberspace, television, streaming – all of them forms of transmission that could not have been imagined when Beethoven lived. And as historians, critics, and biographers gave way to new generations, the changing cultural background put their writings in a new framework, even if this framework was not always acknowledged.

Beethoven Biographies and Related Works,
c. 1870–1927

In a comprehensive bibliography of writings about Beethoven, for the year 1870 we read:

> Understandably, in the year 1870, the whole cultural world celebrated the hundredth anniversary of the great man in many ways. Hundreds of notices appeared in periodicals, and commemorations were held in Bonn and Vienna, the two major Beethoven cities, then in other provincial places, and in untold smaller places.[3]

These centennial publications included minor books on his life and works; one in French by the otherwise unknown H. Barbadette, others in German by the equally forgotten W. Fricke and C. F. Jahn. One that is still worth a look is Ludwig Nohl's compilation entitled *Beethoven-Brevier*. But the flood

---

[3]   *Bibliotheca Beethoveniana; Versuch einer Beethoven-Bibliographie von Erich Kastner, Zweite Auflage mit Ergänzungen und Fortsetzung von Theodor Frimmel* (original edition, Vienna, 1925), published with a reprint of Nottebohm's *Thematisches Verzeichnis* (Leipzig: Breitkopf & Härtel, 1925).

that poured forth in 1870 included at least one that deserves
to be remembered, namely Wagner's essay, *Beethoven*,
which is as important for what it reveals about its author
as for what it says about its subject. Without any claim to
completeness, here is a list of Beethoven biographies of
significance in German, French, and English published
between 1870 and 1927.

Alexander Wheelock Thayer *Ludwig van Beethovens Leben*,
    translated into German by Hermann Deiters (TD) Vol. 1,
    1866 and later volumes down to 1908;
Theodor Frimmel *Ludwig van Beethoven* [compact
    biography]
Romain Rolland *Vie de Beethoven* [a short biography]
Jean-Christophe [Rolland's most famous novel, in part a par-
    able using portions of Beethoven's life as its basis]
Alexander Wheelock Thayer *Ludwig van Beethovens Leben*,
    revised by Hugo Riemann and published in five volumes
    in 1908–1917 (TDR)
Vincent D'Indy *Beethoven: Biographie critique*
Paul Bekker *Beethoven*
Wolfgang Thomas-San-Galli *Beethoven*
Gustav Ernest *Beethoven: Persönlichkeit, Leben und Schaffen*
Ludwig Schiedermair *Der junge Beethoven*
Arnold Schmitz *Beethoven*
J. W. N. Sullivan *Beethoven: His Spiritual Development*

Thayer's Later Contributions, 1867–97

Thayer was never able to publish his biography in English
and in fact he never completed his magnum opus. Its later
publishing history is a web of complexities.[4] His original

---

[4] A first survey of the publication history of Thayer's biography
    was provided by Henry Edward Krehbiel in the Introduction to
    his edition of the work (New York: The Beethoven Association,

version was translated into German, edited by the Bonn
scholar Hermann Deiters and published in three volumes
in 1866, 1872, and 1879. In these volumes Thayer covered
Beethoven's life up to about 1816. The remaining years had to
be filled in by later editors in both the German and English
editions, that is, Riemann, Krehbiel, and Forbes, and accordingly these later versions differ markedly in their treatment
of Beethoven's last decade.

In a letter to George Grove in 1892, Thayer lamented
his condition, telling Grove that his eyes were weak, that
he was fairly worn out, and that he now feared that writing
the full biography, including the late years, would be beyond
his strength.[5] In fact this problem had been coming on for
many years, as we see from a letter to Deiters of 20 April
1876:

> ...I am still, as I have been for two months, on the year
> 1815, simply because my abominable official and other
> duties take up so much time, and my old trouble with my
> head has plagued me so much...[6]

It's more than likely that Thayer's ailments and inability
to make further progress on his great project were highly
colored by his awareness that in Beethoven's last years
some of the composer's personal relationships and business dealings with publishers were unsavory (above all the

---

1921), vii–xvi. It should be compared with the account by Elliot
Forbes in the Preface to his later edition (Princeton: Princeton
University Press, 1964), v–xvii.

5   *The Life and Letters of Sir George Grove...*, ed. Charles L.
Graves (London: Macmillan, 1903), 390. Grove had been in
correspondence with Thayer since 1864 and esteemed him very
highly as a Beethoven scholar.

6   Quoted here from Bellofatto, *Thayer*, 394, apparently from the
original but no exact reference is given, as with many other
documents in Bellofatto's book.

guardianship struggle over nephew Karl).[7] In the same letter
to Deiters of 1876 he writes that he is unable to decide

> How much of ... Beethoven's character as a man I shall
> make known or suppress... But Beethoven grew to be
> such an unpleasing character in his last years, that I am
> in a very painful dilemma as to how much of the truth to
> tell...[8]

Whatever the reasons, the full biography did not emerge
in his lifetime. Volume II, covering the years from 1795 to
1806, came out in 1872, and by this time Thayer was fighting
chronic headaches. And after Volume III, up to 1816, Thayer
could go no further.

After Thayer's death in 1897 Deiters obtained his papers
and hoped to finish the project. In 1901 he brought out a
revised version of Volume I, in which he added commentary on Beethoven's works, and other material. Then came
Volume IV, dealing with 1817–23, but Deiters died just
before it was published in 1907. At this point the polymath
Hugo Riemann was brought in to finish the job, and from
1908 to 1917 Riemann worked to produce the five-volume
set that became "Thayer-Deiters-Riemann," (TDR), the
standard biography in German for later times. Riemann's
insertions and changes were notable, especially his musical
commentary, but he also regrouped material in the light of
the discovery of new letters and he worked to clarify some
issues that had formerly been unclear.

The task of bringing the whole project into English, at
long last, was then undertaken by Henry Edward Krehbiel
(1854–1923), a well-known American music critic. Krehbiel

---

[7] *Ibid*. See also Maynard Solomon, "Sonneck and Krehbiel: A
Beethoven Correspondence." in Lewis Lockwood and Phyllis Benjamin, eds, *Beethoven Essays: Studies in Honor of Elliot
Forbes* (Cambridge: Harvard University Department of Music,
1984), 66f.

[8] *Ibid*.

had been in contact with Thayer during the last ten years of Thayer's life, and also had Thayer's material available to guide him in writing about Beethoven's last years. He also writes of having had some contact with Deiters. Krehbiel finished his translation in 1914 but owing to wartime conditions the book was not published until 1921.

His main idea was to restore Thayer's intention to provide a rigorous account of the life, in much detail, but not to comment on the music in critical terms. Yet new problems arose, since Krehbiel evidently cut down the narrative in various places, removed appendices, omitted some letters, and paraphrased others. Above all – and understandably – he felt free to deal with the last decade of Beethoven's life in his own way.[9] As he writes in his preface, Krehbiel's aim was to write the concluding chapters "in the spirit of the original author."[10]

And then, in the 1950s, Elliot Forbes re-edited the entire biography and published it in 1964 as *Thayer's Life of Beethoven*.[11] Forbes reworked the whole project once more, again with a view to restoring Thayer's intentions. He removed earlier additions by Deiters, Riemann, and Krehbiel, and supplied new notes and comments which reflected Beethoven scholarship that had been done in the intervening decades. Forbes restored Thayer's main text as much as possible for the years in which we have Thayer's narrative. But for the last decade of Beethoven's life there was now a new problem, since Forbes had to work without Thayer's posthumous papers. Somehow they had been lost

---

[9] For an evaluation of Krehbiel's work see Elliot Forbes's preface to TF, x–xvi.

[10] Krehbiel, TK, preface, vii.

[11] TF.

since Krehbiel had access to them – and these papers still have never been located.[12]

We come back now to Thayer's later years. During this time Thayer lived on in Trieste as United States Consul until he resigned the post in 1882. Apart from two return visits to America in 1871 and 1880 he remained in Europe, keeping up his strong interest in his research, traveling to Germany and England, and contributing essays to *Dwight's Journal* along with other writings.[13] By now, despite the continued influence of Schindler in German circles, Thayer had become the accepted authority on the factual aspects of Beethoven biography, the primary source of knowledge for both writers and readers in this domain. In 1889 the house in which Beethoven had been born in Bonn was purchased by the newly founded Beethoven Verein, with Joseph Joachim as its Honorary President, and in May 1890 the birthplace became the Beethoven Museum. In that year Thayer was made an Honorary Member.[14]

In these last years, despite his physical ailments, he produced some other writings. They included a book on *The Hebrews and the Red Sea* (1883), which he followed in 1892 with a second volume entitled *The Hebrews in Egypt and their Exodus*.[15] In 1876 he lectured to the Schiller Verein of Trieste on Beethoven, and the text became his essay entitled *Ein Kritischer Beitrag zur Beethoven-Literatur* ("A Critical Contribution to the Beethoven Literature"), published in 1877 in Berlin. In the earlier part of the lecture he subjected

---

[12] I should mention here that my own introduction to Beethoven biography took place in a graduate seminar given by Elliot Forbes in 1954 while he was a member of the Princeton Music Department and was working on his revision of Thayer, which came out ten years later.

[13] For a portrait of Thayer in these last years see Bellofatto, *Thayer*, Chapter 15.

[14] For details see *Ibid.*, 277–286.

[15] On these writings see *Ibid.*, 263ff.

a number of fictional tales about Beethoven to withering
scorn, but made sure to give his views on one or two serious
biographical subjects, mainly his objections to still-current
beliefs in Beethoven's supposedly bad relationship to his
brothers Carl and Johann, which had been promulgated by
Schindler.[16]

The last portion of *Ein Kritischer Beitrag* shows a personal side of Thayer as an American that deserves notice.
He begins by comparing two great men who frequently
resorted to humor in their daily discourse – two men who
would be totally unlikely to come to mind in the work of any
other Beethoven scholar or anyone else, but who stood high
in Thayer's estimation – Abraham Lincoln and Ludwig van
Beethoven. He writes as follows:

> It has been shown by competent observers that the great
> President Lincoln could not have dealt with the immense
> responsibilities that pressed upon him without his
> penchant for wit and harmless jokes, which gave him a
> needed refreshment of the spirit. Certainly Beethoven's
> great calamity, his deafness, was only of a personal nature,
> and his goal, as he himself often said, was the fulfillment
> of his art. The great captain of the fate of a nation and the
> sublime master of instrumental music, have in common
> the same element of character – an inclination to humor
> and joking.[17]

Comparing Beethoven and Lincoln, Thayer must have meant
to bring the image of the greatest American president of the
age to his German readers, but also he must have known
very well that this essay would find its way into *Dwight's
Journal*, as in fact it did that same year. And so it would give

---

[16] Published as *Ein Kritischer Beitrag zur Beethoven Literatur*
(Berlin: W. Weber, 1877). As pointed out by Bellofatto, *Thayer*,
249 n. 1, the essay was translated in *Dwight's Journal of Music* in
the issues of November 10 and 24 and December 3 and 22, 1877.

[17] German Edition, 44.

American readers a feeling for the human and personal side of two heroic men. Thayer gives examples of Beethoven's wit and humor, and then closes the text with some general remarks on the Beethoven literature of "the second half of [this] century," noting as usual that countless factual errors about Beethoven continued to appear in books and essays. He ends with a tribute to the late Otto Jahn, who "twenty-five years ago collected material for a Beethoven biography with praiseworthy industry but died before he could complete it." And Thayer closes this elegiac essay by writing:

> In the want of such a work [a complete Beethoven biography], complete and authentic, it may be forgiven me for thinking it my duty to come forward against the deep-rooted, wide-spread errors current in relation to the great composer, and to establish the truth so far as my knowledge and powers enable me to do so...[18]

German Biographers, c. 1870–1935

Theodor Frimmel (1853–1928)

Trained as an art historian, Theodor Frimmel began as a curator at the Imperial Natural History Museum in Vienna, a post he held until 1893. Thereafter he ran a gallery and taught art history at the Vienna Atheneum. But by the 1880s he had gravitated to the world of Beethoven. His first book, *Beethoven und Goethe: Eine Studie* appeared in 1883, followed five years later with a set of essays entitled *Neue Beethoveniana*.

In 1901 he published his short but still highly readable biography, simply entitled *Ludwig van Beethoven*. Frimmel remarks in his foreword that "there are many large and small, old and new accounts of Beethoven's life, but none that in our time offers a comprehensive short overview,

---

[18]   Cited from Bellofatto, *Thayer*, 250.

based on thoroughly researched material, along with many illustrations."[19] His book is indeed a model concise biography, and it was enriched, as Frimmel points out, by his having had access in the 1870s to testimony from a few of Beethoven's contemporaries who were then still living – including Gerhard von Breuning, August Artaria, and C. F. Hirsch. He covers the main phases of Beethoven's career in short chapters, adds portraits and a few facsimile pages from autograph manuscripts, and ending with a short but pithy section that documents each segment of the biography. In the third and fourth editions of 1907 and 1912, respectively, Frimmel added an appendix that amplifies the earlier editions of the book, and also a review of the biographical literature that shows his critical reading.[20] For him Wegeler-Ries is "indispensable," and Schindler is "an important guide, whom however one should not follow blindly." Recognizing Thayer's command of his material, he sees Thayer's biography (and by the time of this addendum Frimmel had seen the whole book) as "a major work... [which] contains a valuable mass of critically handled material..."[21] Frimmel is highly critical of A. B. Marx, and is cautiously favorable to Nohl, of whose work he says, with a hint of disdain, "some of it is valuable."

In later years Frimmel became a full-time Beethoven scholar, interested in every aspect of the subject, publishing separate collections of essays and of Beethoven's letters and a useful volume of contemporary portraits. Taking on a leadership role, he edited a short-lived *Beethoven Jahrbuch* that ran from 1909 to 1911, and finally completed his work

[19] Theodor Frimmel, *Ludwig van Beethoven*, 4th edn (Berlin: Schlesische Verlagsanstalt, 1912), 1.

[20] The appendix is on pp. 88–102, and adds material to each phase of Beethoven's life and work; the review of the Beethoven literature is on pp. 102–3.

[21] Frimmel, *Ludwig van Beethoven*, 103.

with his *Beethoven-Handbuch* (1926), a reference book in two volumes that is packed with extended essays on many vital subjects.[22] Arranged in alphabetical order, it includes entries on individuals in Beethoven's world; on each of the major genres and many individual works, plus other topics. For example, an article on "Schrift" [Handwriting] is one of the very first attempts to sort out some of the idiosyncrasies of Beethoven's verbal and musical handwriting, written long before Beethoven's sketches and autographs became a lively international field of study. Frimmel's "Handbook" is still a basic reference tool for Beethoven enthusiasts, and it is only regrettable that it was never translated into English. It stands beside its successor, *The Beethoven Compendium* of 1991, compiled by Barry Cooper and three other scholars, which brings valuable new material on many Beethovenian subjects. But nevertheless it does not wholly supersede the one-man achievement that is Frimmel's large and interesting handbook compiled sixty-five years earlier.[23]

Paul Bekker (1882–1937)

Among German music critics in the early twentieth century none was more prolific than Paul Bekker. His major book on Beethoven, of 1912, went through many later editions plus an English translation that came out in 1925. Bekker was a critic for two Berlin newspapers (1906–09 and 1909–11), later for a newspaper in Frankfurt and for other journals. In the 1920s he was also an opera *intendant*, first at Kassel then at Wiesbaden, and was a proponent of new music by

---

[22] Theodor Frimmel, *Beethoven-Handbuch*, 2 vols. (Leipzig: Breitkopf & Härtel, 1926); reprinted in one volume by Georg Olms Verlag (Hildesheim, 2003).

[23] *The Beethoven Compendium*, ed. Barry Cooper with contributions by Barry Cooper, Anne-Louise Coldicott, Nicholas Marston, and William Drabkin (London: Thames and Hudson, 1991).

Hindemith, Schönberg, Schreker, Weill, and Krenek. In 1934, the rise of the Nazis forced him to emigrate to the United States, where he continued to write for a German-language journal. Bekker died in New York in 1937.

Prior to his *Beethoven*, Bekker had produced monographs on lesser figures – one on the German composer Oscar Fried (1907), another on Jacques Offenbach (1909). And after 1911 he turned out three more books on musicians: Franz Liszt (1912), Franz Schreker (1919), and Richard Wagner (1924). But he also kept up a stream of other publications from 1912 to 1936, on music and politics, aesthetics, opera, and related subjects.

Bekker's *Beethoven* is a critical overview of Beethoven's creative life, not a factually oriented biography. Designed for the music-loving public and not for specialists, it crosses a dividing line in the history of major books on Beethoven – the line that separates the inner world of Beethoven scholarship from the ever-expanding literature intended for everyman, for listeners and readers who are not concerned with the inner structural aspects of music but are content to absorb serious music as emotional and aesthetic experience. In the preface to his book Bekker writes about Thayer and Nottebohm as follows:

> Sincere admiration for the groundbreaking work of these two men [Thayer and Nottebohm] may not suppress the realization that the fruitful study of a phenomenon like Beethoven can lie first of all in the fusion of all the resulting materials into an artistically fashioned presentation...[24]

Accordingly, Bekker offers a single chapter on "Beethoven the Man," a biographical summation that needs less than seventy-five pages out of a total of more than 600. The bulk of the book is on "Beethoven the tone-poet." At the end he adds a succinct chronological table, year by year, and a parallel

---

[24] Paul Bekker, *Beethoven* (Berlin: Schuster & Loeffler, 1912), vii.

table of the main works in the primary genres. All this shows knowledge of the basic facts, but no interest in probing more complex biographical issues. An example is his discussion of the "Immortal Beloved" letter, which for Bekker remained "undated, lacking in place or year of writing, and allows for the widest guesses as to whom it may have been written."[25] He speculates on possible addressees, including Magdalene Willman, Giulietta Guicciardi, and Therese Brunswick, but leaves it at that, and in general downplays the importance of the whole matter of Beethoven's yearning for a loving relationship with a woman as being subordinated to his ambitions as a composer. Similarly, Bekker deals with the deafness crisis of 1802 and the Heiligenstadt Testament in two brief paragraphs (pp. 28f) but makes no attempt beyond the most obvious to link the events of the life to the works.

From here on the works dominate. Bekker's primary heading for all of his discussions is the "poetic idea," a term he borrows from Schindler, who had ascribed it to Beethoven in a passage that mesmerized biographers for years afterward.[26] Taking Beethoven's late-period use of the term "Tondichter" ["tone-poet"] strongly to heart, Bekker describes what he takes to be the poetic content of many major works. For Carl Dahlhaus, Bekker's writing is "celebrated for the subtlety of language Bekker uses to attempt to put into words the expressive character of musical themes and motives."[27] On the other side, in Bekker's lifetime, we see the oncoming and powerful protagonists of rigorous analysis, above all Heinrich Schenker. To Schenker, Bekker's approach is musical thinking gone wrong as he succumbs to the siren song of verbal poetics instead of penetrating into the tonal content of Beethoven works – and doubtless, those of the other masters of the classical tradition from Bach to Brahms.

---

[25] *Ibid.*, 63.
[26] Brenner, *Schindler*, 254ff.
[27] Dahlhaus, *Beethoven: Approaches to His Music*, 239.

Bekker was in fact one of Schenker's principal *bêtes noir* among all those whom he attacked in his analytical writings. In 1920, Schenker severely criticized Bekker, with others, in his analytical edition ("Erläuterungsausgabe") of the piano sonata Opus 101, again in his analysis of the Fifth Symphony, and from then on the two of them found occasion to launch verbal missiles at each other. Two years later Bekker even found a way to deprecate Schenker's facsimile edition of the autograph manuscript of the "Moonlight" Sonata, and Schenker wrote a long and scathing reply that was not published in Schenker's lifetime but has recently been made available in English in William Drabkin's complete translation of Schenker's *Der Tonwille* essays of 1921–24.[28]

Thomas-San-Galli; Ernest; Schmitz; Riezler

As Beethoven biography became a literary genre for music-lovers and the general concert-going German public in the late 19th and early 20th century, writers alert to its prospects began to flourish. I distinguish here, as before, between Beethoven specialists such as Frimmel, or musicologists who could and did ask basic questions about the state of knowledge in this field, on the one hand – and on the other hand generalists and popularizers who were seeking a place on the shelves of the many who wanted to know more about Beethoven, his life and works, and to have a book on him alongside their volumes by and about Goethe and Schiller.

Two of these writers were Wolfgang Alexander Thomas-San-Galli (1874–1918) and Gustav Ernest (1858–1941).

---

[28] Heinrich Schenker, *Der Tonwille: Pamphlets in Witness of the Immutable Laws of Music: Offered to a New Generation of Youth*, edited by William Drabkin and translated by him and by Ian Bent, Joseph Dubiel, Joseph Lubben, William Renwick, and Robert Snarrenberg, 2 vols. (Oxford: Oxford University Press, 2004–2005). Schenker's previously unpublished essay, "Music Criticism," translated by Drabkin, is in Volume II, pp. 161–5.

From the former (who surely has the most complex name in the annals of Beethoven scholarship) we have two books of interest. The first was his effort to identify the "Immortal Beloved" as Amalie Sebald, a singer whom Beethoven indeed met at Teplitz in 1811 and again in 1812 (the year of the "Immortal Beloved" letter). But although Beethoven exchanged some affectionate notes with her, two months later, in September of 1812 when he returned to Teplitz, Thomas-San-Galli's claims for her as the recipient of the famous letter have long since been dismissed.[29]

His second book on Beethoven, his biography of 1913, is a solid example of what had now come to be a standard model of the genre. By "standard model" I mean a narrative that covers his youth in Bonn, then the first years in Vienna up to 1802 and the Heiligenstadt Testament, followed by the "middle Beethoven" and finally the "late Beethoven." As Thomas-San-Galli makes clear, he aims to provide a "a straightforward, readable Beethoven biography" in contrast to Frimmel's very slim volume and to the multi-volume products of "at least twenty-five years ago," including the books by Wasielewski, Nohl, and Marx, along with Schindler and, by now in 1913, the five-volume Thayer-Deiters-Riemann. In a footnote Thomas-San-Galli mentions that, just as his book had gone to the printer, there appeared the "aesthetic Beethoven work" by Bekker.

From Gustav Ernest, a musician who also wrote on Wagner, Brahms, and the German composer Wilhelm Berger, came a sizeable Beethoven biography in 1920, reprinted many times. Like that of Thomas-San-Galli, it was aimed at the general public, with no claims to any special scholarly discoveries, but one can see that Ernest had absorbed Thayer and Nottebohm, to both of whom he makes reference throughout.

[29] See Solomon, *Beethoven* (1998), 214.

Arnold Schmitz (1885–1923)

A prolific writer on several fields of music history, Schmitz studied at Bonn University with Schiedermair and later taught there, which helps account for his editing a volume of essays for Schiedermair's sixtieth birthday in 1937.[30] In the 1920s Schmitz brought out four major publications on Beethoven. The first was his interesting *Beethovens Zwei Prinzipe*, (1923), an attempt to distinguish "two principles" of thematic organization in Beethoven's works, which I mentioned earlier in the segment on Schindler.

Schmitz then followed in the jubilee year 1927 with a general book, simply entitled *Beethoven*, and a more ambitious study of the Romantic image of Beethoven.[31] The latter was a searching and well-informed study of Beethoven's relationship to the Romantics, but its main focus is on his prevailing image of him as it emerged in the nineteenth century, with its culmination in Wagner. His book is influenced by the concept of "political Romanticism," as developed by the notorious political theorist Carl Schmitt, the nationalist writer whose work he cites at several points.[32] Many years later, Maynard Solomon reviewed the abiding question of whether Beethoven can be properly seen as a Romantic composer, that is, not only as the forerunner of the later Romantics but their father-figure – or as, fundamentally,

---

[30] Arnold Schmitz, *Beethoven und die Gegenwart* (Berlin & Bonn: Dümmler, 1937).

[31] Arnold Schmitz, *Beethoven* (Bonn a. Rhein: Verlag der Buchgemeinde, 1927); and idem, *Das romantische Beethovenbild: Darstellung und Kritik* (Berlin and Bonn: Dümmler, 1927).

[32] Schmitz, *Das romantische Beethovenbild*, 61, 70, 73, 118, 178. See Helmut Loos, "Arnold Schmitz as Beethoven Scholar: A Reassessment," *Journal of Musicological Research*, 32/2–3 (2013), 150–62. Loos claims (p. 153) that Schmitz "was quite untouched by any National Socialist disposition," a viewpoint that I am unable to either confirm or deny.

an artist rooted firmly in the Classical tradition, as Charles Rosen presents him in his influential book, *The Classical Style*.[33] The issue becomes the more complex the deeper one goes into Beethoven's development, from the early works that clearly stem from his absorption of Mozart and Haydn – through the powerful compositions of the second maturity (from the *Eroica* to the Eighth Symphony and from the Opus 18 quartets to the innovations of Opus 74 and 95); and finally to the last phase, with the late piano sonatas and the late quartets, the most deeply philosophical music of its own time or – perhaps – any time.

Walter Riezler (1878–1965)

With Riezler we come to a more original contributor to this growing literature. Trained in art history like Frimmel, Riezler studied with Max Reger, was a founding member of the *Deutscher Werkbund* (a forward-looking art center) in 1907, and from 1910 director of the Municipal Museum in Stettin. Forced out by the Nazis in 1933, he was unable to emigrate, turned to full-time work in musicology, and the result was his singular *Beethoven* book of 1936.[34] After World War II, he was given an honorary professorship at the University of Munich (1946) and other honors, and produced two more books: *Einheit der Künste* (1947) and *Schuberts Instrumentalmusik* (1967). Although its publication date (1936) might perhaps suggest some possible hint of conformity to the cultural programs of the Nazi regime,

---

[33] Maynard Solomon, "Beyond Classicism," in his *Late Beethoven: Music, Thought, Imagination*. (Berkeley: University of California Press, 2003), 27–41.

[34] Walter Riezler, *Beethoven* (Berlin and Zurich: Atlantis Verlag, 1936 and later editions; the English translation by G. D. H. Pidcock (New York: Dutton, 1938, reprint 1972) is serviceable but omits many important elements in the original German edition).

in power since 1933, the fact is that there is no trace in Riezler's book of anything of the kind, and there is much within
it that implicitly rejects any such association – or, for that
matter, any cultural biases except those we should expect
from a protagonist of pure music, or "absolute music," as
Riezler puts it in a major heading.[35] His approach diverges
from the biographical mainstream up to this time, German
and other, in its resolute devotion to music as an art-form.
The central focus is on the works and their structural organization, not on their personal or contextual backgrounds,
which are given minimal space. The book is organized in
three parts plus a lengthy appendix; the discussion of the
works is much longer than the sections on the life and on
"Beethoven and Absolute Music," which are of about equal
length. The appendix is nothing less than a thirty-four page
analysis of the first movement of the *Eroica*.

Striking in Riezler's book is the paucity of references to
earlier biographers, even to Thayer, who hardly appears, nor
to Nottebohm, who is absent. On the other hand, Riezler is
the only generalist writer in the German Beethoven literature of the 1930s who makes frequent references to Heinrich
Schenker, from his Ninth Symphony monograph of 1912 to
his later writings, up to and including Schenker's lengthy
analyses of the Fifth Symphony and the *Eroica*.[36] Riezler was
not sympathetic to Schenker's later work, with its layered
concepts of musical structure, "middle ground" and "foreground," which he found beyond his ken, but his comments

---

[35] That his book was published in Zurich, not in Germany, may
    reflect the possibility that his favorable references to Schenker,
    a Viennese Jew, would not have been permitted by a German
    publisher. But this is simply a hypothesis.

[36] Heinrich Schenker, *Das Meisterwerk in die Musik*, Vol. III,
    (Munich: Drei Masken Verlag, 1930). The analysis of the Fifth
    Symphony is in *Der Tonwille*, 1,5, 6; see Drabkin's translation.

on the earlier Schenker essays set him apart from the bet-
ter-known Beethoven commentators of his time.[37]

The French Tradition: Romain Rolland; Vincent D'Indy; others

We turn now to the parallel traditions in Beethoven biography in France and in England between 1870 and 1945.
Again, this special field, as cultivated by French and English writers, should be seen within the larger frameworks
of their national cultural histories and musical landscapes,
their ways of depicting Beethoven in his own right and
in his importance in their own musical worlds. And both
French and English commentators had also to reckon with
Beethoven as a major artist of the past who could be said to
transcend national boundaries but who was, nevertheless, a
German cultural idol. The larger backdrop, needless to say,
is deeply colored by the immense tragedy of Europe during
this period of two world wars: of France's invasion by Germany both in 1914 and again in 1940, of the atrocities of the
Holocaust, of the entrance of the United States into World
War II in 1941 after Pearl Harbor, and the eventual return of
peace in 1945 that launched a new era. We can hardly be surprised to see French writers and intellectuals dealing with
Beethoven as a primarily German cultural idol, along with
other exemplars of German art, literature and music fully
in mind, aware of the ambivalence of German politics and
culture. The historian Fritz Stern cites a comment attributed
to Charles de Gaulle about the German people in 1945 at the
end of World War II:

> ...amid the ruins of Stalingrad he [de Gaulle] muttered to
> an aide, 'Quel peuple!' The translator later inquired, 'You
> mean the Russians?' 'No,' said de Gaulle, 'the Germans.'

---

[37] On Riezler's view of Schenker's work see schenkerdocuments
online.org, s.v. "Riezler."

And Stern continues:

> The general's lapidary judgment at that place of devas-
> tation says much about the German drama of the past
> century, which he grasped clearly. He was referring to the
> people who had thrice attacked his [de Gaulle's] coun-
> try, whose power had corrupted and nearly destroyed
> historic Europe, and who were guilty of genocidal crime
> unique in Europe's history. But he also knew that the
> German people had been prodigiously creative and that
> they would be indispensable for the postwar recovery
> of Europe. He grasped the deep ambiguity that hovers
> around German greatness.[38]

After the famous Habeneck performances of Beethoven's
symphonies in the late 1820s, and in later years, there were
few limits to the admiration in which Beethoven was held
by French composers, critics, artists, and the musical public.
For Hector Berlioz, by far the most original creative figure
in French music in the earlier part of the century, Beethoven
was an eagle who could fly at altitudes far above any other
birds, and he remained, as one commentator has put it, "the
most substantial presence in Berlioz's artistic world."[39] At
mid-century the myth-making surge was also given support
by French writers, including Balzac and Victor Hugo, as well
as by leading musicians. In his appraisal of the impact of
Beethoven on French thought and feeling, Leo Schrade cites
a passage from Hugo's *Shakespeare*:

> As for Germany, the matrix, like Asia, of races, hordes,
> and nations, she is represented in art by a sublime man...
> That man is Beethoven. Beethoven is the German soul.[40]

---

[38] Fritz Stern, *Five Germanies I Have Known* (New York: Farrar,
Straus and Giroux, 2006), 3.

[39] D. Kern Holoman, Introduction to Hector Berlioz, *A Critical
Study of Beethoven's Nine Symphonies*, translated by Edwin Evans (Urbana: University of Illinois Press, 2000), vii.

[40] Schrade, *Beethoven in France*, 83.

The story of Beethoven in France has been amplified and re-interpreted by several scholars, including Beate Angelica Krauss.[41] As she observes, published writing on Beethoven in France was focused more on criticism and appreciation than on biography, which is hardly surprising at this early stage of limited access to Beethoven documents, which French enthusiasts were not likely to undertake. We remember that in 1839 Wagner's friend Gottfried Engelbert Anders had translated Wegeler-Ries into French, a year after its original publication, and Krauss notes that there were two other similar French translations in 1839 and 1862.[42] And although Schindler's biography had been translated into English almost as soon as it appeared, there is no record of any translation into French. Wide-ranging attempts to come to grips with Beethoven the man, along with commentary on the works, had to wait until the early twentieth century, with Vincent D'Indy and Romain Rolland. And even then the subject was strongly weighted towards the works rather than the life, although with these two writers they were approached from opposed standpoints.

Vincent D'Indy and Romain Rolland, born fifteen years apart, were cut from entirely different cloth. Rolland (1866–1944) began as a music historian, then expanded his interests to become one of the most famous French intellectuals of his time. As a recent article puts it, he was well known "as historian, critic, biographer, playwright, and polemicist [who] ranged inexhaustibly over a wide field of intellectual activity..."[43]

[41] Beate Angelica Krauss, *Die Beethoven-Rezeption in Frankreich: Von Ihren Anfangen bis zum Untergang des Second Empire* (Bonn: Beethoven-Haus, 2001); and her article, "L'homme et l'Oeuvre? Der französische Beethoven," *BBS* 4 (2005), 71–89.

[42] *Ibid.*, 72.

[43] Robert Henderson, "Rolland", in Sadie and Fortune, *The New Grove*.

Of all Beethoven biographers Rolland is the only one who was awarded a Nobel Prize or, surely, considered for one. He received the prize for his famous novel, *Jean Christophe* (1904–12), an allegorical novel about a composer who is a fictional version of Beethoven, placed within the modern world of the French fin-de-siècle. Rolland's early work had been on the origins of the modern lyric theater, and after his rise to fame as a novelist and essayist he returned to his lifetime Beethoven project. He had published a short *Vie de Beethoven* in 1903 in a periodical (and in book form in 1907), and it was surprisingly influential in its time, stressing Beethoven as an artist whose work embodies ethical as well as aesthetic values.[44] Rolland followed with books on Tolstoy and Mahatma Ghandi, and in his later life became a well-known pacifist. From 1927 to 1944 Rolland produced his major Beethoven study in seven volumes, entitled *Beethoven: Les grands époques créatrices*. Incorporating his own hand-written music examples (they also appear in the English translations of the first two volumes – the only ones that were published in English), Rolland's prose embraces his appraisal of the artistic qualities of the major works. For Rolland this was the centrally important issue, not to recount details of the life and not to explore structural or analytical matters, but to give the world his conception of the magnitude of Beethoven's achievements, and their intrinsic importance.

Vincent D'Indy (1851–1931), on the other hand, was an ultra-conservative composer within the orbit of the classical tradition as it had been defined for the French by César Franck. In his time D'Indy composed operas and instrumental works, some of which are still performed, such as his "Symphony on a French Mountain Air." But he was also

---

[44] For a recent overview see Stefan Hanheide, "Die Beethoven-Interpretation von Romain Rolland," *Archiv für Musikwissenschaft* 61/4 (2004), 255–274.

a prolific writer, and his subjects included musical pedagogy and books on Franck (1906), Beethoven (1911), Chabrier and Dukas (1920) and Wagner (1930). Living through the age of Fauré, Debussy and Ravel, and still present in the 1920s to witness the transformational achievements of Stravinsky and Schönberg, D'Indy looked to the past with blinders on. His outlook is summed up in what he taught his students at the Schola Cantorum, that "the sonata form of Beethoven was the ideal form for the expression of abstract music."[45] And yet, some of his critical comments on particular works are still worth reading today.

A few words on two other French contributors. One is Jacques Prod'homme, a noted musicologist, who wrote a book on the Beethoven symphonies (1906) in which some biographical material is interwoven. He also published other books on Beethoven, including a collection of accounts of Beethoven by his contemporaries (1927), a book on the piano sonatas (1944), and a volume on the "Immortal Beloved" problem. All this amid other works on a variety of musical figures, including Mozart, Berlioz, Gounod, Gluck, Liszt, and Wagner, plus other well-known historical figures, including Voltaire and Napoleon.[46]

The other is the politician Edouard Herriot (1872–1957), a national figure who was three times prime minister of France but still found time to write a Beethoven biography (1929). Perhaps only in France could one find an intellectual who could conduct an active and successful public career on this level but who also had the ambition and background that could enable him to write a book of this kind.

---

[45] Edward Lockspeiser, "Vincent d'Indy and Beethoven," *The Listener*, 7 October 1954, 48.

[46] http://en.wikipedia.org./wiki/Jacques-Gabriel Prod'homme

The English Tradition: George Grove; Donald Francis Tovey; Marion Scott; J. W. N. Sullivan

Though Beethoven never traveled to England he had a long and cordial relationship with some of its publishers and patrons, and he was always aware of their great interest in his works. As Alan Tyson pointed out, among the first to introduce his music there was William Gardiner (1770–1853), an amateur musician who performed Beethoven's String Trio Opus 3 in the early 1790s, shortly after it had been composed.[47] Around 1814 Gardiner wrote to Beethoven and spoke of the "originality and beauty" of that work and of his subsequent efforts "to procure your compositions, as much as the war would admit."[48]

Beethoven was in touch with English publishers from 1807 onward, and, as Tyson writes, "after 1809 there are few of his major works which he did not try to dispose of in England."[49] His contact with the Edinburgh publisher George Thomson had begun even earlier, in 1803, and lasted nearly two decades, leading to his prodigious output of arrangements of Scottish and other folksongs.[50] From 1813 to 1824 Ferdinand Ries was in England, and during these years he acted as a virtual agent for Beethoven. English visitors to Beethoven in the later years included Sir George Smart, an important British conductor; Charles Neate, who came to know Beethoven beginning in 1815; and Cipriani Potter, a

---

[47] Alan Tyson, *The Authentic English Editions of Beethoven* (London: Faber & Faber, 1963), 14.

[48] Gardiner's letter is available in Beethoven's *Briefe* No. 764, with further particulars on the dating of his early performance of Op. 3.

[49] Tyson, *The Authentic English Editions*, 14.

[50] See Barry Cooper, *Beethoven's Folksong Settings* (Oxford: Oxford University Press, 1994), for a comprehensive overview of this branch of Beethoven's work.

pianist and composer who visited Beethoven in 1817. All of these musicians were connected with the Philharmonic Society, which began in 1813 and quickly became a platform for the performance of Beethoven's symphonies. As a recent writer puts it, "...out of the eighty concerts given during the society's first decade (1813–22) only twelve did not contain at least one of Beethoven's works."[51] Another important figure in the Beethoven cult was Ignaz Moscheles (1794–1870), a prominent pianist and composer, who lived in London from 1825 to 1846, before moving to Leipzig. Moscheles had been close to Beethoven in Vienna from 1810 on, made the piano score of *Fidelio* in 1814, and remained a lifelong admirer. His translation of Schindler in 1841 helped to spread Schindler's work beyond any other early biography.[52]

Accordingly, Beethoven's ascendance in English musical life began early and continued to flourish throughout the nineteenth century and beyond. As for musical commentary, however, including biography, it was slow to develop, and it took time for scholars to go beyond other subjects of national interest, above all the continental composers who had spent significant time in England – Handel and Mendelssohn. While my present remarks are no more than a sketch of the subject, "Beethoven in England," it is clear that a primary gathering point for Beethoven commentary and for musical erudition in the later nineteenth century was *Grove's Dictionary of Music and Musicians* in 1879 – the first comprehensive reference book of its kind in English.

---

[51] Clive, *Beethoven and His World*, 263 (in the article "Philharmonic Society").

[52] See Mark Kroll, *Ignaz Moscheles and the Changing World of Musical Europe* (Woodbridge: The Boydell Press, 2014), especially Chapter 5, "Encounters with Beethoven and His Music."

George Grove as Beethoven biographer

George Grove (1820–1900) was trained as a civil engineer, but in later life his interests broadened into biblical studies and music.[53] In 1856 he began writing program notes for the concert series at the Crystal Palace, a famous exhibition hall designed to be a showcase for British culture and manufactured goods of all kinds, which had opened in 1851 to tremendous acclaim.[54] Grove wrote program notes for Crystal Palace concerts for more than forty years, and his notes on the Beethoven symphonies became the basis for his later book on them, published in 1896 and still being reprinted in our time.[55] For the first edition of his *Dictionary* Grove wrote many articles on composers, including Beethoven, Mendelssohn, and Schubert, expanding on his own favorites and showing modern interest in continental music. As a critic remarked long afterward, "In the original 'Grove' Beethoven, Schubert, and Mendelssohn *each* had more pages than Bach, Handel and Haydn put together."[56]

Reading George Grove's 1879 article on Beethoven is still rewarding, both for content and style. It has the length and substance of a small book in itself, running to 47 double-column pages, and it is well-informed and shows awareness of the best in Beethoven scholarship as it stood in the late 1870s. Grove's judgements on issues in both life and works

[53] On Grove see Percy Young, *George Grove 1820–1900: A Biography* (London: Macmillan, 1980), and the useful precis in Sadie and Fortune, *The New Grove*, Vol. 7 (1980), 752–55.

[54] On the Crystal Palace see, most recently, David Cannadine, *Victorious Century: the United Kingdom, 1800–1906* (New York: Viking, 2017), 276–82.

[55] See *The New Grove*, 7, 753.

[56] These three articles were later published in book form with the title *Beethoven, Schubert, Mendelssohn*, ed. Eric Blom (London: Macmillian, 1951). My quotation is from a review of the book in *The Musical Times*, Vol. XX (1951), 312.

are thoughtful and persuasive. He shows solid knowledge of the writings of Thayer and Nottebohm that were then available, he reviews the career of Beethoven in careful detail, and he closes this very substantial contribution with comments on the Beethoven literature that are very much worth reading. Thus Grove on Nohl and Thayer:

> Nohl is said to be inaccurate, and he is certainly diffuse, but I for one owe him a debt of gratitude for his various publications, the information in which can be found nowhere else... Last and best is the 'Ludwig van Beethovens Leben' of A. W. Thayer (Berlin, 1866, '72) of which the 3rd volume is on the eve of publication and which, through the caution, wide research, and unflagging industry of its author has already taken a place far higher than any of its predecessors...[57]

Although Grove's original Beethoven article was inevitably replaced in later editions, it remains a model of intelligent and well-informed biography. It shows none of the romanticism that colored the work of his continental contemporaries, such as Nohl, for whom Beethoven was a figure-head of growing nationalism; or others like Bekker whose portrayals of the works were wreathed in Romantic imagery and language. It is not surprising that Grove and Thayer became close colleagues, and their correspondence shows strong evidence of their mutual intellectual respect and affinity.

Donald Francis Tovey as critic and biographer

In the history of modern music criticism on the higher level, Donald Francis Tovey (1875–1940) holds a place of distinction. In Joseph Kerman's words,

---

[57] George Grove, "Beethoven" in idem, *A Dictionary of Music and Musicians (A.D. 1450-1889)* 4 vols., (London and New York: MacMillan, 1879–90), Vol. 1, 203.

Tovey must still be the most widely read music critic in English-speaking countries. His work has been attacked; it has also been bypassed and tacitly contradicted; but it has never lost its broad appeal[58]

To Kerman's encomium I can add my own, since my own youthful introduction to vivid and stirring writing about serious music was with Tovey's *Essays in Musical Analysis* that I found in my public library in New York in the 1940s.[59] His allegiance to the classical masters was unwavering, and though it reflects the Victorian era in which he grew up, it is unsurpassed for its vivid qualities. As Kerman also notes, Tovey's later reception was dimmed in the rising world of music theory and analysis, as exemplified by Schenker and other, principally German, thinkers. But Tovey's sharpness of perception, his sometimes quirky and oblique style, his insight into musical process, and his ability to synthesize complex issues in a few words – all this puts Tovey in a class by himself among the English critics of the first half of the twentieth century.

But what of biography? In his posthumous book on Beethoven, of 1944, Tovey showed his true feelings when he wrote this passage:

To study the lives of great artists is often a positive hindrance to the understanding of their works; for it is usually the study of what they have not mastered, and thus it undermines their authority in the things which they have mastered.[60]

Yet two pages later he praises "two books [that] have saved me from the trouble of attempting either a new biography

---

[58] Joseph Kerman, "Tovey's Beethoven," in *Beethoven Studies 2*, ed. Alan Tyson (Oxford: Oxford University Press, 1977), 172.

[59] See my *Beethoven: The Music and the Life*, xvii.

[60] Donald Francis Tovey, *Beethoven*, (Oxford: Oxford University Press, 1944), 1.

or a philosophic account of his relation to his age" – these two are the biography by Marion Scott (1934) and J. W. N. Sullivan's *Beethoven: His Spiritual Development* (1927). As Tovey declares, "dealing with the music as music is more than enough for me."[61]

Yet three decades earlier Tovey had agreed to write the article on Beethoven for the famous Eleventh edition of the *Encyclopedia Britannica* (1910–11), and in a short span of six double columns he had provided pithy and provocative comments on topics in Beethoven biography. Here are his headings:

> 1) Parentage and Childhood; 2) First visit to Vienna (1787); 3) Biographical Sources; 4) Relations with Haydn [including comments on Mozart]; 5) Rising Fame and Popularity; 6) Deafness; 7) Anxieties; 8) Character; and then, continuing on Beethoven's works, he writes on 9) The Three Styles; 10) Evidence of the Sketch-books; 11) First Period Works; 12) Boldness and Breadth; 13) Beethoven's Rubicon [the "Waldstein" Sonata]; 14) Central Masterpieces; 15) The Third Period; 16) New Fugue Forms; 17) Supreme Artistic Concentration; 18) Immeasurable Influence.

This article and others that Tovey wrote for the *Britannica*, including his piece on Mozart, were tacitly omitted from his collection entitled *Musical Articles from the Encyclopedia Britannica* (1944), presumably in keeping with Tovey's wishes. But it still could be made available as a biographical essay, even now, and it would do him credit. A few nuggets will show what I mean:

> [On "Biographical Sources"]: Thayer, rescuing Beethoven's character from the sentimental legends which had substituted melodrama for life, dealt unflinchingly with the facts, until the mass of grotesque and sometimes sordid detail only threw into clearer light the noble

---

[61] *Ibid.*, 3.

character and passionate zeal for the higher moral ideals throughout every distress and temptation to which a hasty and unpractical temper and the growing shadow of a terrible misfortune could expose a man.

[On "Deafness"]: …his art and his courage rose far above any level attainable to those artists who are slaves to the 'personal note,' for his chief occupation at the time of this document [the Heiligenstadt Testament] was his 2nd symphony, the most brilliant and triumphant piece that had been written up to this time.

Marion Scott

The biography by Marion Scott to which Tovey gave praise is nowhere near as interesting as his own little encyclopedia article. Her book, a good example of what I am calling the "standard version," is about evenly divided between an overview of the life, which raises no important questions but records the basic facts and gives a survey of the works, by genre. The book by Sullivan is another matter, however, and no survey of major writings on Beethoven can overlook it.

J. W. N. Sullivan: *Beethoven: His Spiritual Development* (1927)

This is one of the most widely read books on the composer ever written. Sullivan (1886–1937) was primarily a mathematician and science writer with broad interests, and at one time he was deputy editor of *The Athenaeum*, directed by John Middleton Murry. His main publications were almost all on scientific subjects, aimed at a broad public, but Sullivan also had contacts with prominent literary figures, including Aldous Huxley, who became a close friend, and T. S. Eliot as well as others.[62]

---

[62] For a recent precis of Sullivan's career and a critical appraisal of his work, see Kevin Korsyn, "J. W. N. Sullivan and the *Heiliger*

Sullivan's *Beethoven* is the work of a highly intelligent generalist in music. Its main strength lay in Sullivan's ability to drive home a central truth, namely that Beethoven's works reflect spiritual states that were fundamental to his nature as an artist. As Kevin Korsyn has shown, Sullivan's view of Beethoven, reacting against a view of music as pure aesthetic experience, argues eloquently for the belief that great art is intrinsically the product of a moral vision, and that

> The greatest function of a work of art is to present us with a higher organization of experience... Beethoven's work will live because of the permanent value to the human race, of the experiences it communicates.[63]

It goes without saying that any approach to music through analytical or formal avenues is anathema to Sullivan, who even goes so far to say that:

> Beethoven's profoundest attitude towards life, as expressed in his music, owes nothing to the mediation of his intelligence. The synthesis of his experience that is achieved by a great artist proceeds according to laws of which we know almost nothing, but purely intellectual formulation plays a very small part in it.[64]

Though nothing could be further from his purpose than writing a factual biography, Sullivan traces his thesis from Beethoven's early years to his last works, with the deafness crisis of 1798–1802 as the manifest turning point. From here

---

Dankgesang: Questions of Meaning in Late Beethoven," *BF* 2 (1993), 133–176.

[63] J. W. N. Sullivan, *Beethoven: His Spiritual Development (a Study of Greatness)*, London and New York: Knopf, 1927, 137. Also see Korsyn, "J. W. N. Sullivan," 139 for parallel statements and for evidence of Sullivan's indebtedness to the critical work of I. A. Richards.

[64] *Ibid.*, 143

on for Beethoven, the Wegeler letters and the Heiligenstadt Testament show the emergence of the defiant artist,
"defending his creative power" and sensing that "his genius,
that he had felt called upon to protect, was really a mighty
force using him as a channel or servant."[65]

Perhaps most telling for Sullivan's approach is his
exclusion from "the main line of Beethoven's spiritual development" of all those works that do not conform to his thesis.

> Such works as the fourth, sixth, and eighth symphonies
> depict states of mind that require no such intensity of
> realization. It is significant that they were all written
> comparatively quickly and that each of them accompa-
> nies, as it were, one of his greater works.[66]

On their having been composed quickly Sullivan is out
of his depth, since sketchbook evidence shows that at least
the realization of the Sixth and Eighth symphonies took as
long as did the evolution of the Fifth and Seventh. For the
Fourth, completed in 1807 we are less sure, owing to the loss
of sketches in 1806, but there is no basis beyond an act of
faith for the claim that Beethoven's experience in composing
the Fourth, Sixth, and Eighth symphonies was of a significantly lower order of importance to him – and to us – than
the writing of the Third, Fifth, and Seventh. As I have put it
elsewhere:

> Somehow one feels that this statement [Sullivan's claim
> that these works are 'not in the main line of Beethoven's
> spiritual development'] is both true and untrue. It seems
> true in the sense that the 'heroic' works, which are cer-
> tainly pathbreaking, may well have partly emerged as
> responses to the composer's personal crises; it seems
> untrue in insisting that the 'other' works are of a lesser

---

[65] *Ibid.*, 59.
[66] *Ibid.*, 87.

order of importance because no similar claim can be made for them...[67]

What does not fit Sullivan's "heroic" model is the idea that Beethoven could embrace the aesthetic domains of beauty, subtlety, irony, and complexity as readily as he could the aesthetic of power and the overcoming of tragedy and despair in works such as the *Eroica* and the Fifth and Ninth symphonies. For, in Beethoven's so-called "heroic period," by now the most familiar term for the second period of his creative life, between about 1803 and 1812, he not only composed the Fourth, Sixth, and Eighth symphonies, but also other works that probe regions other than the powerful and the heroic. They include the Violin Concerto, the Fourth Piano Concerto, the Cello Sonata Opus 69, the Trio Opus 70 No. 2, the Quartet Opus 74, the "Archduke" Trio, and the Violin Sonata Opus 96, all of which are "primarily lyrical, intimate, and expansive."[68]

Yet despite my cavils, Sullivan's book remains a classic statement of its kind, an interpretation of a major aspect of Beethoven's lifetime achievements that brings important truths to a wide public. This is true even if it goes too far, as I see it, in asserting its thesis to the exclusion of a wider and more comprehensive point of view.

[67] Lewis Lockwood, "Beethoven, Florestan, and the Varieties of Heroism," in Scott Burnham and Michael P. Steinberg, eds, *Beethoven and His World* (Princeton: Princeton University Press, 2000), 38.

[68] *Ibid.*, 39.

9. Paul Bekker.

10. Romain Rolland, Agence de presse Meurisse.

11. Sir George Grove, Elliot and Fry.

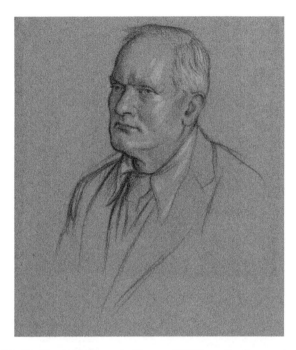

12. Sir Donald Francis Tovey, William Rothenstein.

13. J. W. N. Sullivan, Lady Ottoline Morrel.

4

Beethoven Biography and European Politics, 1933–77

German Beethoven Scholarship in the Nazi Period (1933–45)

GERMAN WRITINGS ABOUT BEETHOVEN between 1933 and 1945 directly reflect the nation's descent into the nightmare of the Nazi regime. From Hitler's rise to power until the collapse of the Third Reich in 1945, his cultural ministers promoted Beethoven as a symbol of national prestige, and the state apparatus did all it could to manage and manipulate his public image. In keeping with party doctrines, his stature as a great German composer and a "Nordic hero" was publicized by the organs of party propaganda, and any aspect of his life and work that seemed to contradict the party line was forgotten or suppressed – such as the Flemish origins of his family.[1] Even the Ninth Symphony, with its setting of Schiller's "Ode to Joy" and profession of faith in human brotherhood, was reinterpreted along party lines. Thus Hans Joachim Moser, an avowed Nazi sympathizer, could argue that Schiller's "kiss to the whole world" couldn't really mean "a desire to fraternize with every Tom, Dick, and Harry, ...but must have meant a humanity conceived in as German terms as possible."[2] And recent scholarship

---

[1] David Dennis, *Beethoven in German Politics, 1870–1989* (New Haven: Yale University Press, 1996).

[2] *Ibid.*, 152.

has documented the ways in which the Beethoven-Haus in Bonn, the primary German center of Beethoven scholarship, surrendered to the Nazi regime's demand that Beethoven be reincarnated as a true German hero, not as a believer in the rights of man and of human brotherhood, as in fact he was.[3]

We need no reminder in the twenty-first century that in musicology and every branch of the arts and sciences, rampant German antisemitism of the early 1930s drove many Jewish musicians and intellectuals into exile, many of them coming to the United States if they were able to get there. And of course a vast number of German Jews were systematically deprived of all their rights and property and sent to their deaths in the extermination camps in what remains the most monstrous ideological crime in modern history.

Against this background, the story of critical and biographical commentaries on Beethoven may seem to be a lesser issue within the tortured history of German intellectual life under the Nazi regime. But because Beethoven's works were powerful and important for all Europeans – Germans, Jews, and everyone else – it may help to remember that for the victims of the regime, playing and hearing his works could be, in the worst circumstances, a momentary experience of hope. We know that this was true, for example, in the Łódź ghetto in 1942, where, as I have described it elsewhere, a symphony orchestra of the Ghetto dwellers managed to play a series of concerts, including the Fifth Symphony. As an eye-witness describes it, the conductor's

> yellow Star of David quivered on his right shoulder when Ryder [the conductor] swayed to the music... the

---

[3] See *Ibid.*; and among other recent studies, Pamela Potter, *Most German of the Arts: Musicology and Society from the Weimar Republic to the End of Hitler's Reich*. (New Haven and London: Yale University Press, 1998); and Patrick Bormann, *Das Bonner Beethoven-Haus 1933–1945* (Bonn: Verlag Beethoven-Haus, 2016). The list could easily be extended.

deliverance motif thundered majestically throughout the hall, and conductor Ryder seemed to be carried away in this finale. In that instant, one felt, almost bodily, the experience of future salvation.[4]

If we take the long view, it's clear that Beethoven as cultural icon had begun to be assimilated into politics more than a century earlier, in fact during his lifetime, as at the Congress of Vienna. Over the decades, the power of his music and his fame as a defiant artist who overcame disability were made to symbolize the aspirations of the long-desired German national identity. As David Dennis writes, "Since his lifetime – especially after 1870 – every major interest in Germany claimed this composer and his music to be symbolic of its particular vision of the German future."[5]

This aspiration underlies some of the German biographies I have been considering, as far back as Schindler. Nor would it be surprising to find that, although Thayer was respected for his diligent research, more than a few of his German readers in the late nineteenth and early twentieth centuries would have thought it appropriate that his work should appear in their language and be completed by his German editors, first Hermann Deiters and then Hugo Riemann, rather than accept that the father of Beethoven biography should have been an American.

Since cultural life in these years was defined by the implacable ideological and racial doctrines of the New Order, commentators had to cope with some facts that did not fit Nazi ideals. One of these, we saw, was the evidence of Beethoven's Flemish ancestry. Another was his physical appearance. For the fact is that the real Beethoven looked nothing like a blonde and blue-eyed Aryan hero, with his

[4] Lewis Lockwood, *Beethoven's Symphonies: An Artistic Vision* (New York: W. W. Norton, 2015), 225–39, citing the chronicle by Oskar Rosenfeld.

[5] Dennis, *Beethoven in German Politics*, 6.

short stature, his gray-blue eyes (according to one contemporary source), and his wild hair – as we see from many
contemporary depictions.[6] But, as Dennis puts it,

> For a mass audience, the propaganda method of the
> 'big lie' sufficed: the *Volkischer Beobachter* [the main
> Nazi news vehicle] simply insisted that Beethoven was
> of Aryan descent and justified its position by misrepre-
> senting contemporary descriptions and portraits of him.[7]

Lending an official stamp to the Nazi version of the Beethoven image was the work of those German Beethoven
scholars who furthered their careers by embracing the Nazi
myths of racial and supremacist politics. Among them, most
conspicuously in the 1920s and then throughout the Nazi
period, was Ludwig Schiedermair (1876–1957).

Ludwig Schiedermair

From 1927 to 1945 Ludwig Schiedermair was the leader of
the Beethoven-Archiv in Bonn.[8] He was active in German
musicology throughout the Nazi years, gaining academic
appointments and honors for his work on Mozart and Beethoven. His *Der junge Beethoven* (1925) is a detailed survey of
the composer's youth and early manhood in Bonn.

---

[6]   *Ibid.*, 135; and for the images, Comini, *The Changing Image of
      Beethoven*, passim.
[7]   *Ibid.*, 135.
[8]   The Beethoven-Haus as a museum in Beethoven's birthplace
      had been founded in 1890, but the scholarly archive came into
      being only in 1927. On Schiedermair's role in the Beethoven-
      Archiv and its publications, see Bormann, *Das Bonner Beet-
      hoven-Haus*, 8–29 and passim; pp. 344f. provide an extensive
      list of Schiedermair's publications, from 1900 to 1957. For a
      brief summary of Schiedermair's role in creating the Nazi im-
      age of Beethoven, see Dennis, *Beethoven in German Politics*,
      139 and other references.

As Patrick Bormann points out, the book shows aspects of Schiedermair's well-attested antisemitism in his brief discussion of the status of the Jews in Bonn in the eighteenth century, just as it also anticipates his later attempt to whitewash the well-documented alcoholism of Beethoven's father Johann – this latter point was troublesome for the approved Nazi version of Beethoven's allegedly strong German upbringing.[9]

Werner Korte

Beethoven's "Germanness," as the Nazi ideologues promoted it, is writ large in books that came out at this time. Composer biographies had of course been a long-established category when the Nazis took over in 1933, and they did what they could to bend it to their purposes. In the words of Ernst Bücken, editor of a series of musician biographies, the writing of such works was "a task dictated by the new times."[10] His Beethoven volume, published in 1936, was penned by Werner Korte (1906–82), a pro-Nazi who could be counted on to conform to party doctrines.[11]

As Korte says, his aim is to "correct the errors into which the standard portrait of Beethoven had been thrown by Bettina von Arnim and Schindler, and to give his readers an antidote to the 'programmatic' interpretations of prewar times." By "programmatic" he was probably alluding to the "poetic" interpretations by Paul Bekker and others, and

---

[9] Bormann, *Das Bonner Beethoven-Haus*, 116f. and 118–33 on antisemitism at the Beethoven-Haus throughout the Nazi years; 120 and 173 on Schiedemair's denials of Johann's alcoholism as a long-term condition.

[10] Potter, *Most German of the Arts*, 221. Her book contains other references to Korte, his activities and his antisemitism.

[11] Werner Korte, *Beethoven: Eine Darstellung seines Werkes* (Berlin: Max Hesses Verlag, 1936).

what he substitutes are elementary formal descriptions of a number of works.[12]

But what is mainly of interest in Korte's book is not what is in it but what is not. Biographical details are kept to an absolute minimum, thus avoiding all the usual problems of Beethoven's ancestry, appearance, and troubled life; the primary purpose is to discuss the works, in fairly simple formal exegesis. Entirely missing is any discussion of Beethoven's belief in Enlightenment ideals and his awareness of Kantian idealism. Korte does refer to his lifetime desire to set Schiller's "Ode to Joy", but there is no reference to its original phrase, "Beggars will become brothers of princes," which Schiller later changed to "All men shall become brothers." Suppressed as well is Beethoven's resistance to the repression of free speech in Austria, first during the Napoleonic wars and later under Metternich. And it goes without saying that when Korte comes to Beethoven's song cycle "An die ferne Geliebte," there is no mention of the fact that the poetic text was the work of Alois Jeitteles, a young Jewish medical student and poet in Vienna.

East Germany and West Germany, 1945–77

With the end of World War II in 1945 "an era was over and a new Europe was being born." Thus wrote the late Tony Judt in his informative book on postwar Europe.[13] Political and cultural changes were taking place on a drastic scale both East and West when the Iron Curtain came down and separated the Western democracies from the then Soviet Union and its satellite states, lasting until the dissolution of the Soviet bloc in 1989. And with regard to a cultural figure as prototypically German as Beethoven, differences

---

12 *Ibid.*, v.
13 Tony Judt, *Postwar: A History of Europe since 1945* (New York: Penguin Press, 2005).

in viewpoint between West Germany (the *Bundesrepublik)* and East Germany (the *Deutsche Demokratische Republik*) were bound to be conspicuous and significant.

Recent studies of music and history in East Germany, an avowedly socialist but manifestly repressive political regime, show patterns of reception attuned to the political climate in which traditional German art and music was cultivated and managed by the regime.[14] Elaine Kelly puts it this way in commenting on how Beethoven and Goethe, as German classics, were seen in the GDR over these years:

> The heroic narratives in which they had been situated in the 1950s were decidedly incongruous in later years... as the Enlightenment ideals of the state came under scrutiny so did the reputations of the period's illustrious figureheads. Yet, if the construct of the heroic Beethoven had lost its relevance, Beethoven himself had not. In the years surrounding his 200th anniversary in 1970, artists in East Germany like their counterparts in the Federal Republic, began to explore aspects of the composer that were incongruous with the heroic model, focusing in particular on the late Beethoven.[15]

For Beethoven biography and scholarship in both Germanies and in Austria, the conferences that were held in 1970 and 1977 can help to provide a focus. These conferences were showcases for scholars active in this period, and we also recognize that some of their participants, in both East and West Germany and in Austria had formerly been fellow travelers with Nazi organizations. And yet, looking back, we can also perceive the gradual internationalization of Beethoven studies, as German specialists were beginning

---

[14] A succinct overview is in Dennis, *Beethoven in German Politics,* Chapter 5, "Germany Divided and Reunified"; more recently, Elaine Kelly, *Composing the Canon in the German Democratic Republic* (Oxford: Oxford University Press, 2014).

[15] Kelly, *Composing the Canon,* 102f.

to recognize English and American contributions. We can begin with Austria and its center in Vienna.

Austrian Beethoven Conferences, 1970 and 1977

Two Beethoven conferences were held in Vienna in honor of the bicentennial year 1970, a generation after Austria's liberation but with the long shadow of the country's history still hanging over events of this kind. The first took place in December 1969 under the auspices of the Austrian Academy of Sciences, and its proceedings were published in 1970 in Vienna and edited by Erich Schenk.[16] Schenk (1902–74) was a prominent musicologist in the Austrian scene, who held the post of Ordinarius Professor at the University of Vienna from 1940 until his retirement in 1971. Formerly a member of Nazi academic organizations, Schenk had evidently collaborated in identifying Jewish students, and worked with Herbert Gerigk on the notorious *Lexikon der Juden in der Musik* ("Dictionary of Jews in Music") – all of which did not prevent his continuing his academic career in Vienna after World War II and gaining honors.[17]

Although in Schenk's foreword to the 1970 proceedings he calls it an "Internationale Beethoven-Symposium," he defends the restriction of the meeting to German and Austrian scholars with the explanation that "[contributions were] requested from outstanding professionals from those lands that in the master's life and art were directly or

---

[16] *Beethoven-Studien: Festgabe der Oesterreichischen Akademie der Wissenschaften zum 200. Geburtstag von Ludwig van Beethoven*, ed. Erich Schenk (Vienna: H. Böhlaus, 1970).

[17] Wikipedia, "Erich Schenk," which includes a section on "Erich Schenk and Antisemitism;" on the *Lexikon* see Eva Weissweiler, *Ausgemerzt! Das Lexikon der Juden in der Musik und seine mörderischen Folgen* (Cologne: Dittrich, 1999).

indirectly connected to him", meaning Germany and Austria.[18] One of the papers presents biographical material, namely Beethoven documents from Viennese archives; another describes the music library of Archduke Rudolph. Others dealt with Beethoven's music and earlier traditions; with *Fidelio*; with idiosyncrasies of notation; and – far afield but Austrian – on Bruckner's notes about the Third and Ninth Symphonies. There are no analytical papers, no sketch studies, but also no focus on political or ideological issues.

The parallel meeting in Vienna, the *Beethoven-Symposion Wien 1970* included Germans, Swiss, Poles, Italians and others, and one American participant, Warren Kirkendale, then at Duke University, who had been a student of Erich Schenk in Vienna. Kirkendale's paper dealt with traditional elements in the *Missa Solemnis*, and was related to his earlier book on fugue in classical chamber music.[19]

Seven years later, in 1977, a very different Beethoven conference was sponsored in Vienna, this time by the *Österreichische Gesellschaft für Musik*. This gathering brought a wider international array of speakers, including Beethoven specialists, was focused on "documentation and performance practice." It breathed an air of openness to the outside world, with participants from Germany and Austria, but also from Denmark, England, and the United States,

---

[18] "…das Wort von ausgezeichneten Fachleuten aus jenen Ländern erbeten, denen der Meister in Leben und Kunst mittel- oder unmittelbar besonders verbunden war." *Beethoven-Studiened. Schenk*, 7.

[19] *Beethoven-Symposion Wien 1970* (Vienna: Hermann Böhlaus Nachfolger, 1971); Warren Kirkendale, "New Roads to Old Ideas in Beethoven's *Missa Solemnis*," *Musical Quarterly LVI* (1970), 665–701; and his *Fugue and Fugato in Rococo and Classical Chamber Music*, 1966, rev. edn, translated from the German edition by Margaret Bent and the author (Durham: Duke University Press, 1979).

including myself and my esteemed colleague Richard Kramer.[20] The published volume brought new research, notably
Peter Stadlen's paper on "Beethoven and the Metronome," in
which he identified some of Schindler's forgeries in the conversation books that he, Stadlen, had discovered and made
known earlier in BBC broadcasts of 1971.[21] Scholars from the
Beethoven-Haus included Emil Platen, Hans Schmidt, Shin
Augustinus Kojima, Siegfried Kross, and Sieghard Brandenburg. And most striking, in the Viennese context, were
the papers by Otto Biba, on Beethoven and concert life in
Vienna in 1807–08; and by Franz Eibner on "Criteria for the
Perception and Interpretation of Beethoven's Work," which
really meant melodic and analysis of form along Schenkerian lines. Eibner's use of Schenkerian analytical procedures
and his recognition of Schenker's importance as a theorist
was something that had been entirely missing from the 1970
Austrian conference as well as, so far as I know, from Austrian musicology and pedagogy in general.

Bonn, Berlin, and Detroit, 1970 and 1977

Bonn, 1970

In these same commemorative years there were also two
international Beethoven conferences in both Germanies,
West and East. The first was held in Bonn in September of
1970, sponsored by the *Gesellschaft für Musikforschung* (the
primary German musicological society). It was on an enor-
mous scale, with more than 170 papers, mainly on Beethoven
but also other topics, and with participants from Germany
and Austria but also the United States, England, Italy, Israel,

---

[20] Jens Peter Larsen, Denmark; Peter Stadlen, England; the United States, Richard Kramer and myself.
[21] *Beethoven-Kolloquium 1977*, ed. Rudolf Klein (Kassel: Bärenreiter, 1978), 57–75.

Poland, Russia, Japan, and other countries; the congress report ran to more than 700 pages.[22] With this gathering, mid-to-late twentieth-century Beethoven scholarship was in full display, and new perspectives emerged in Beethoven biography and criticism.

Even now, almost fifty years later, when the digital world provides access to sources on a scale that could not have been dreamed of in 1970, I doubt that the massive content of the Bonn 1970 conference report, in all its details, has been fully absorbed into the general Beethoven literature. The wealth of topics was vast and a few were on other subjects, but Beethoven research was the main line. One paper of special value I will single out here was by Emil Platen, on Beethoven's autograph manuscripts.[23] If this paper had not been buried in a conference report it could have been the impetus to an important body of research showing late-stage compositional changes in Beethoven's works beyond the sketch stage. As it happens, Platen and I had been pursuing this issue entirely independently, and his paper took note of an early essay of mine along the same lines.[24] His paper offered important insights into Beethoven's changes in several movements of the Opus 59 Quartets, and pointed the way to valuable studies of quartet autographs by Richard Kramer and Sieghard Brandenburg, ten years later.[25] It sug-

---

[22] *Bericht über den Internationalen Musikwissenschaftlichen Kongress Bonn 1970*, ed. C. Dahlhaus, H. J. Marx, M. Marx-Weber, and G. Massenkeil (Kassel: Bärenreiter, 1971).

[23] The German title was "Beethovens Autographen als Ausgangspunkt morphologischer Untersuchungen," pp. 534–6.

[24] Lewis Lockwood, "On Beethoven's Sketches and Autographs: Some Problems of Definition and Interpretation," *Acta Musicologica* 42 (1970), 32–47; reprinted in my *Beethoven: Studies in the Creative Process* (Cambridge, MA: Harvard University Press, 1992).

[25] Christoph Wolff, ed., *The String Quartets of Haydn, Mozart and Beethoven: Studies of the Autograph Manuscripts* (Harvard

gested lines of new research that have still to be adequately developed, even in our time.

Berlin, 1970

In that same December of 1970 a parallel meeting was held in East Berlin, sponsored by the "Committee to Honor Beethoven in the German Democratic Republic 1970." As might be expected, the speakers were mainly East German but many also came from Eastern Europe, including several from Russia. Nor is it surprising that more than a few papers dealt with political subjects that reflected current official DDR doctrines. Thus Israel Nestjew's paper, "Musik Beethovens in Sovjet Russland," ("Beethoven's Music in Soviet Russia"), or Ernst Hermann Meyer's "Das Werk Ludwig van Beethovens und sein Bedeutung für das sozialistisch-realistische Gegewartsschaffen" ("The Work of Beethoven and its Importance for the Socialist-Realist Production of Today"). And yet the winds of change were faintly blowing, as in contributions by scholars working within the inner orbit of historical scholarship with minimal or no ideological purposes or inflections. They included Nathan Fishman (USSR) whose edition of Beethoven's "Wielhorsky" Sketchbook had been published eight years earlier, in 1962. Fishman's edition of this important sketchbook of 1802–03 was and is of lasting value to Beethoven scholarship. It is the key sketchbook for Beethoven's major works and new ideas in the crucial period of 1802 and early 1803, the time of the Heiligenstadt Testament and the earliest ideas for what became the *Eroica* Symphony. Fishman's edition is of inestimable value for our understanding of this crucial time in his life and work.[26]

University Department of Music, 1980); Kramer's paper was on Opus 59 No. 1; Brandenburg's on Opus 132.

[26] The sketchbook is located in Moscow, Central (Glinka) Museum for Music Culture, dates from 1802–03, and includes sketches for his Piano Sonata Op. 31 No. 3, the oratorio *Christus am*

1977 Conferences: Berlin, Detroit

By chronological accident, Beethoven's birth in 1770 and death in 1827 give rise to celebrations seven years apart. And so, in 1977 there were three more major conferences, in Berlin, Vienna, and Detroit.

The East German 1977 "International Beethoven-Congress in Berlin" was again promoted by the regime. It opened with remarks by a state minister who stressed Beethoven's "achievements for the common people" as part of the "nature of our socialist state." But in fact the topics now reflected some awareness in the DDR of progress in the broader world of Beethoven scholarship. There were panels on Beethoven's sketches, his social status, and on analysis; and a raft of papers by a wide range of scholars. These included Alan Tyson (UK) and Douglas Johnson (USA), who had already transformed understanding of the manuscript structure of the Beethoven sketchbooks and were on their way to producing, eight years later, with Robert Winter, their pathbreaking book entitled *The Beethoven Sketchbooks: History, Reconstruction, Inventory*.[27] Present too was Maynard Solomon, who gave papers on Beethoven's "class position and outlook" and another on "Antonie Brentano and Beethoven." The latter restated Solomon's thesis that Antonie Brentano was the intended recipient of the famous "Immortal Beloved" letter of 1812. This is, one hardly need say, a subject of intense interest to biographers, and we will come back to it in later discussion of Solomon's work.[28]

Ölberge, and it also contains the earliest sketches for the Eroica Symphony. See JTW, 130–6. Fishman had also presented a paper on the sketchbook at the Bonn 1970 Conference.

[27] Douglas Johnson, Alan Tyson and Robert Winter. *The Beethoven Sketchbooks: History, Reconstruction, Inventory*. (Berkeley: University of California Press, 1985).

[28] Maynard Solomon, "New Light on Beethoven's Letter to an Unknown Woman," *Musical Quarterly* LVIII (1972), 572–87

The Berlin 1977 event also included papers by Dagmar Beck and Grita Herre on the Schindler forgeries in the conversation books, and by Clemens Brenneis on the "Fischhof-Manuskript," an early biographical source. Again, as with the Bonn conference of 1970, this Berlin conference report remains a repository of scholarship that should still be consulted decades later, as much of it deserves to be remembered and utilized in current research.

To close my conference survey, I turn to the Beethoven meeting in Detroit in 1977.[29]

This was a small gathering, with eight papers and two panel discussion reports, one of which was on sketch research. The papers were highly informative. They included an overview of writing about Beethoven by the astute critic Michael Steinberg, and a valuable study of the young Beethoven's 1796 tour of Prague and Berlin, by Douglas Johnson. Other papers included Eva Badura-Skoda on performance conventions; Otto Biba on concert life in Beethoven's Vienna; James Webster on the middle-period quartets; Karl-Heinz Köhler on the conversation books (which he was then editing); Maynard Solomon on Beethoven and Schiller; and Robert Winter on the sketches for the "Ode to Joy". The American setting, with visitors from Austria and from both East and West Germany, was free of ideological overtones.

---

and his later "Antonie Brentano and Beethoven" *Music & Letters* 58 (1977), 153–69, which coincided with the first edition of his *Beethoven* (New York: Schirmer Books, 1977).

[29] *Beethoven, Performers, and Critics: the International Beethoven Congress, Detroit 1977*, ed. Robert Winter and Bruce Carr (Detroit: Wayne State University Press, 1980). See the review by Richard Kramer in *Journal of Music Theory* Vol. 27, No. 2 (Autumn, 1983), 299–306.

5

The Modern Era

The Bicentenary Year 1970:
Two Contrasting Biographies

IT IS NOT MY aim in this book to discuss or even mention all the known Beethoven biographies but to focus on what I take to be the mainstream of the subject. And since the 1970 celebration of the bicentenary of Beethoven's birth stimulated a number of biographies, it seems appropriate to look at two of them before turning to more recent contributions. The two I choose are George Marek's *Beethoven: Biography of a Genius* (1969) and Martin Cooper's *Beethoven: The Last Decade* (1970; 2nd revised edition 1985). They contrast sharply with one another in style, approach, and quality, as will be seen.

George Marek (1902–87) emigrated to the United States from Vienna in 1920. After an early career in advertising he became an executive at RCA Victor, where he produced recordings by well-known musicians including Arturo Toscanini. He also wrote on music for popular journals along with a few other composer biographies before his Beethoven book came out in 1970. Here Marek offered a lively and accessible account of the life, overtly excluding any attempt to deal with the substance of the music but showing some engagement with the Beethoven literature up through the late 1960s.[1] He also reports having "put together" a research

---

[1] See the reviews by Elliot Forbes in *JAMS* 23/3 (1970), 525–529 and by F. E. Kirby in *Notes*, 27/1 (1970), 35–36.

team in Vienna, led by the eminent Haydn scholar H. C.
Robbins Landon, and was able to report some newly found
facts and documents.[2] As a general overview, as matters
stood about 1970, Marek's book could serve as an adequate
introduction to Beethoven biography for the lay reader.

   Martin Cooper's book, *Beethoven: The Last Decade,
1817–1827*, is a much stronger contribution. It was the work
of an experienced British music critic who also wrote on
French and Russian music. As Stanley Sadie remarked,
Cooper's essays show "his unusual ability to discuss a particular topic in a wide cultural context, and his writing… is
marked by clarity and elegance."[3] His book shows what gains
can be reaped from concentrating on a single large sector
of Beethoven's life and work rather than the whole. But it is
not just that Cooper's framework is manageable but that he
covers the territory with care and intelligence, and parts of
his book are still highly useful today. About a third is devoted
to the life, year by year from 1816 to the end, beginning with
the lawsuit over the guardianship of Karl that consumed
Beethoven's energies so deeply in his forlorn quest to create
a rewarding domestic household. The last three chapters
are especially well done; they deal with "Social and political
attitudes"; "General Culture"; and "Religious attitudes and
beliefs." They show wide and careful reading, knowledge of
sources then only partly available, such as portions of the
Conversation Books, the *Tagebuch* of 1812–18, the letters,
and much else. As an appendix, Martin Cooper included
a discussion of "Beethoven's Medical History," by Edward

---

2   George Marek, *Beethoven: Biography of a Genius*, (New York:
    Thomas Y. Crowell, 1969) Foreword. Marek notes that, as mat-
    ters stood in 1970, no Beethoven biography in English had been
    written later than the early 1940s, when John N. Burk's biogra-
    phy had appeared (1943).
3   *The New Grove Dictionary of Music and Musicians* (1980) s.v.
    "Cooper, Martin."

Larkin, which is of value not only for its content but for its own special bibliography on the subject, as up to date as was possible in 1985 when a revised edition appeared.

Maynard Solomon, 1977 and 1998

I turn now to the single modern biography that, forty-odd years ago, took hold of Beethoven's life story as it had been established by Thayer and his successors, and significantly reframed it for readers in our time. I am referring to Maynard Solomon's *Beethoven*, originally published in 1977 and reissued in a revised edition in 1998. Responses to Solomon's work inevitably varied, but there is a consensus that this book was, as Robert Winter put it, "the most heartfelt and brilliant full-length study of Beethoven in more than a hundred years."[4]

Maynard Solomon came to musicology from an entirely different career. In 1950, age twenty, he and his brother Seymour Solomon (1922–2002) founded the record label known as Vanguard Records. Vanguard was one of the primary recording ventures of its time, and it developed an extensive catalogue of recordings of classical music and of folk music and blues. Its performers included Joan Baez, as well as The Weavers and the great Paul Robeson, who had been blacklisted for his left-wing political views. These choices were consonant with Maynard Solomon's strong interest in progressive politics and in the writings of Marx and Freud, interests that are visible in his publications from the 1970s on. In 1973 he edited a selection of readings entitled *Marxism and Art*, and in later years he was associated with the psychoanalytic periodical *American Imago*. He also edited a volume of essays in honor of the literary critic Harry Slochower, who had taught at Brooklyn College but

---

[4]   Robert Winter, review in *Notes of the Music Library Association* 34 (1978), 849.

was fired from his position there in 1952 when he refused to testify before a U.S. Senate Internal Security subcommittee as to whether he had ever been a Communist.[5] Solomon included another tribute to Slochower in the preface to his *Beethoven Essays* of 1988.[6]

This broad range of interests is reflected in Solomon's Beethoven biography, which remains a fundamentally important contribution in our time. Enriched by his knowledge of psychoanalysis and Marxist aesthetics, the book surprised many a reader with his interpretations of some of the most emotionally laden episodes in Beethoven's life. Among them were the deafness crisis and its first culmination in the Wegeler letters of 1801 and the Heiligenstadt Testament of 1802, as well as Beethoven's later legal battle over his nephew Karl. To these and other difficult situations Solomon brought highly original insights. One was the Freudian concept of the "Family Romance" (by which Beethoven "replaced" his hapless father Johann van Beethoven with an imagined father of noble status). Another is the idea of the "Nobility Pretense," in which Beethoven imagined himself to be of noble lineage, as in the instance in which this champion of the common man was angered when his guardianship case was assigned to a court for commoners rather than the nobility.[7] To which I will add

---

5   Slochower won reinstatement in 1956 when the Supreme Court ruled that he had been denied due process of law – and was then suspended for allegedly having made false statements at the Senate hearing. See the New York Times obituary for him for his death in 1991 at https://nyti.ms/29ngbTe. I should add that in my own last year as an undergraduate at Queens College (1951–52) Harry Slochower taught a literature course that remains memorable to me.

6   Maynard Solomon, *Beethoven Essays* (Cambridge MA: Harvard University Press. 1988), xi.

7   On the "Family Romance" see Solomon, *Beethoven*, 2nd edn, 28–31 and many later references; on the "Nobility Pretense:"

that Solomon's study of the text and context of the famous letter to the "Immortal Beloved," and his proposal that the likely intended recipient was Antonie Brentano, stands as one of the most brilliant exercises in document interpretation in many years. Though many other theories have been advanced and other candidates, especially Josephine Deym, are still being proposed by various writers, none, in my view, have effectively displaced Solomon's as a convincing explanation.[8]

In a review that I published in 1979, I expressed admiration for the "restless, challenging spirit [with] which [Solomon] attacks sedately established hypotheses and positions, coordinating details into connected patterns and working with the whole in view."[9] Looking back at that review, I would still maintain its premises and conclusions, but if I had it to do over again I would express a wider and deeper sympathy, as I now feel it, for Solomon's treatment of Beethoven's development as a composer. My feelings certainly owe a great deal to my having, in the meantime, written my own Beethoven biography along different lines.

But there is much more to Solomon's contributions to scholarship than his Beethoven biography. He went on from this book to a parallel biography of Mozart (1995) and his Schubert essays would presumably have generated a full-length biography had not illness intervened.

Solomon's essays on Beethoven in musicological journals give more detail about the composer's life than could be accommodated in his book. In addition, he made other

---

see *Ibid.*, 118f., and his essay, "The Nobility Pretense" in Solomon, *Beethoven Essays*, 43–55.

[8]   Solomon, *Beethoven*, 2nd edn, Chapter 15, pp. 207–46; and his *Beethoven Essays*, Ch. 11 ("Recherche de Josephine Deym") and 12 ("Antonie Brentano and Beethoven"). For a summary of the subject and Solomon's views as of 1998 see his *Beethoven*, 2nd edn, 502f.

[9]   My review of Solomon in *19th-Century Music* 3 (1979), 76–82.

important contributions to Beethoven scholarship. One is his edition of the *Tagebuch* of 1812–18, the most important diary of Beethoven's lifetime. Another, which I discussed earlier, is his annotated edition of Gerhard von Breuning's boyhood memoirs of Beethoven's last years, from late in 1825 to his death in 1827, when Beethoven was living in the *Schwarzspanierhaus* ("The House of the Black-Robed Spaniards"), in Vienna.

His edition of the *Tagebuch*, available in three different publications, is a more significant enterprise. This was Beethoven's intimate diary from the years between, roughly, the Seventh and Eighth symphonies and the "Hammerklavier" Sonata. It gives us eloquent evidence of Beethoven's private thoughts during this difficult period. We see in Beethoven's letters that he frequently mingles personal and business matters – but this *Tagebuch* was for his eyes only. It belongs with the Heiligenstadt Testament and the "Immortal Beloved" letter, both of which Beethoven kept locked away in a private drawer and which were discovered after his death. But the *Tagebuch* also reflects his wide reading at the time of writing, and as Solomon writes, it is "unsurpassed as a record of Beethoven's intellectual interests."[10] One of Solomon's discoveries was that, besides reading in Western philosophy, mainly Kant, Beethoven also acquainted

---

[10] Solomon, "Beethoven's Tagebuch of 1812–1818," in *Beethoven Studies 3*, edited by Alan Tyson (Cambridge: Cambridge University Press, 1982), 207. This was the first of Solomon's publications of the *Tagebuch* and presented the German text with English translation. The second appeared in Solomon's *Beethoven Essays* (Cambridge, MA: Harvard University Press, 1988), 233–295, with revised commentary but only in English translation. The third was issued by the Beethoven-Haus in German only, as Maynard Solomon, *Beethovens Tagebuch*, ed. Sieghard Brandenburg (Bonn: Beethoven-Haus, 1990) with numerous facsimiles of pages from the various surviving copies (only a few leaves in Beethoven's own hand survive).

himself with Eastern and Indian spiritual literature, including the *Bhagavad-Gita* and the *Rig-Veda*, which he found in German translations. As Solomon writes,

> Beethoven appears here to be particularly drawn to Eastern and Rosicrucian ideas of purification, asceticism, sacrifice, and the suppression of libidinal interest in the outer world. Perhaps these notions helped to enhance his ability to absorb the shocks of mortality, increasing infirmity, deafness, guilt, and disappointment.[11]

Solomon's contributions are of lasting value for their originality, care in presentation, and enlargement of the whole subject. His biography of 1977/1998 was pre-eminently a penetrating study of the man, a modern, psychologically sensitive biography that followed Beethoven through the vicissitudes of his life. It was not designed to deal with the works in detail but rather to give the reader a vivid sense of who Beethoven was and what he accomplished. Close readers will find that Solomon's endnotes are often as informative as his main text, and that they are scrupulously fashioned. His book challenged accepted explanations, raised new questions, and put Beethoven biography on a new footing.

Kerman, Tyson, and Kropfinger, 1980 and 2000

Articles in reference books are generally conceived as summaries of the accepted general state of knowledge, whether or not they are written by highly qualified authors. But as we saw with George Grove's "Beethoven" for the original *Grove's Dictionary* and Tovey's brilliant article for the *Encyclopedia Britannica*, they can be much more than convenient resumes of the surface information. The two articles I want to discuss in this chapter are important contributions, the more so since their authors, in different ways, were at the

[11] Solomon, "Beethoven's Tagebuch of 1812–1818", 208.

top of their fields and were steeped in knowledge of the subject. And both, the one co-authored by Joseph Kerman and Alan Tyson (1980), in English, and the other, by Klaus Kropfinger (2001), in German, have been issued as independent books.[12]

First, Kerman-Tyson, which first appeared in 1980 in the sixth edition of *Grove's Dictionary*, which was then re-cast under the brilliant editorship of Stanley Sadie and emerged in twenty volumes as *The New Grove*. As a gigantic compendium, which now continues to be updated in its online version, *The New Grove* displaced any earlier music reference book in English and fully competed with its German counterpart, *Die Musik in Geschichte und Gegenwart* ("Music in History and in the Present").[13] For his Beethoven article Sadie turned to two of the most prominent practitioners in the field.

Joseph Kerman (1924–2014) was a central figure in American musicology and over a long career he had a major influence on the larger direction of the field. For Kerman, whom I knew well over many years, there are two sides to traditional musicology. One is focused mainly on the wide-ranging study of the whole sweep of Western music history and musical life in all its phases; the other aims at the aesthetic evaluation and critical interpretation of individual works. Though he was partial to the latter, Kerman, who had studied at Princeton with Oliver Strunk, did distinguished work in music history, first on the English

---

[12] Joseph Kerman and Alan Tyson, *The New Grove Beethoven* (New York: Norton, 1981); and Klaus Kropfinger, *Beethoven* (Kassel: Bärenreiter, 2001).

[13] For a lengthy assessment of *The New Grove* see *The Musical Quarterly*, LXVIII/2 (April, 1982). Virtually the entire issue is devoted to reviews of Grove articles by specialists. The contribution by Bathia Churgin on "Music of the Classical Era" (pp. 228–37) contains comments on the "Beethoven" article under discussion here.

Renaissance, especially the English madrigal school, and later on Beethoven. Yet he was convinced that much traditional scholarship was insufficiently open to critical thought about music. As he put it in a trenchant review of the field, musicologists too often exhibit a "deliberate policy of separating off their musical insights from their scholarly work."[14] Kerman's attack on "positivism" in music scholarship resonated through the 1980s with many younger scholars, and he is sometimes regarded as the progenitor of the "New Musicology."[15] Yet much of what some of its proponents profess and practice goes much further into the realm of the subjective than what we see in Kerman's work, as he tried to stand firmly at the juncture at which historical musicology and criticism might join with one another rather than fly apart. Kerman contributed to both, and was a leading voice throughout his career on the need to fuse them. And another thing that distinguished Kerman from most of his contemporaries was the bite and lucidity of his prose, whatever the subject.

As a Beethoven scholar, Kerman wrote valuable essays. They include his article on the song cycle *An die ferne Geliebte*; another on Tovey's writings on Beethoven; still another on codas in larger works.[16] His larger projects included his well-known book on the Beethoven string

---

14 Joseph Kerman, *Contemplating Music* (Cambridge MA: Harvard University Press, 1985), 18. A valuable review was published by Leo Treitler in *JAMS*, XLII (1989), 375–402.

15 For a sampling of some aspects of what is now a very large field of activity, as it stood fifteen and more years ago, see *The Cultural Study of Music: A Critical Introduction*, ed. Martin Clayton, Trevor Herbert, and Richard Middleton (New York: Routledge, 2003).

16 Kerman, "*An die ferne Geliebte*," in *Beethoven Studies* (1973), 123–57; idem, "Tovey's Beethoven," in *Beethoven Studies* 2 (1977), 172–92; idem, "Notes on Beethoven's Codas," *Beethoven Studies* 3 (1982), 141–59.

quartets (1966) and his critical edition in 1970 of the "Kafka" papers, the largest surviving collection of Beethoven's early sketches, with full facsimiles and transcriptions.[17]

His co-author for the *Grove* article, Alan Tyson (1926–2000), was a brilliant scholar whose contributions on Mozart and Beethoven were of pathbreaking importance. But Tyson also ranged more widely, in these fields and in others. His early education had included training in classics, medicine, and psychology, especially psychoanalysis. He taught psychology at Oxford and was a co-editor of the English translation of the complete works of Sigmund Freud. Thereafter Tyson turned to full-time work in musicology. His first book was on the authentic early English editions of Beethoven (1963), whose importance to textual studies he demonstrated for the first time. He also contributed effectively to the preparation of the first reliable edition of the Beethoven letters, as edited by Sieghard Brandenburg.[18] Later Tyson moved on to highly original analysis of the paper-types and other physical features of the Beethoven sketchbooks and other manuscripts. This enabled him, in collaboration with Douglas Johnson, to present new ways of reconstructing the many sketchbooks that had been dismembered over the years, or from which leaves had been removed by earlier owners.[19] Tyson, with Douglas

---

[17] Ludwig van Beethoven, *Autograph Miscellany from circa 1786 to circa 1799, British Museum Add. MS 29801, ff. 39–162*, ed. Joseph Kerman 2 vols. (London: Trustees of the British Museum, 1970).

[18] See Brandenburg's introduction to the festschrift for Tyson's 65 birthday, entitled *Haydn, Mozart and Beethoven: Studies in the Music of the Classical Period: Essays in Honor of Alan Tyson*, ed. Sieghard Brandenburg (Oxford: Clarendon Press, 1998), v–vi.

[19] See Alan Tyson and Douglas Johnson, "Reconstructing Beethoven's Sketchbooks," *JAMS* 25 (1972), 137–56. This work was also aided materially by Sieghard Brandenburg, in many of his

Johnson and Robert Winter, in 1985, created the first truly comprehensive catalogue of the vast trove of Beethoven sketchbooks, both large-size and pocket sketchbooks, with vital information on their contents, dating, relevant literature, and much more.[20] Thereafter Tyson produced important similar studies of the autographs of Mozart.[21]

Against this background one might think that a close scrutiny of Kerman and Tyson's biographical article for *The New Grove* might be too demanding, since, as they write in the preface to the book version, "the larger space devoted to Beethoven's life than to his work does not reflect any view of absolute priorities, only a view of proprieties for the writing of dictionary articles."[22] But in fact the article repays attention, as it offers a distillation of thought about Beethoven by two highly experienced hands, whose knowledge comes through in many a detail. It is in four parts: Tyson wrote the section on the Life and the last section, on "Posthumous influence and reputation;" Kerman wrote the long section on "The Works" and on Beethoven's "Personal Characteristics."

Tyson's short biography covers the basic chronological story: the family background, the early years in Bonn, the first period in Vienna and then the rise to greatness despite – or in some ways intertwined with – the deafness and all that it brought. The article is a model of its type; pithy, sharply

---

studies of individual works and their sources. Accordingly, the entries under Brandenburg's name in the index to JTW (see my abbreviations list) are more numerous than for any other scholar.

[20] Douglas Johnson, Alan Tyson, and Robert Winter, *The Beethoven Sketchbooks: History, Reconstruction, Inventory* (Berkeley: University of California Press, 1985).

[21] Alan Tyson, *Mozart: Studies of the Autograph Scores* (Cambridge MA: Harvard University Press, 1987).

[22] Joseph Kerman and Alan Tyson, *Beethoven* (New York: W. W. Norton, 1983), ix.

observed, and finely written. Tyson's manner is visible in passages such as this:

> [On the young Beethoven's relationship to Haydn]: "...
> he was almost bound to feel the genius of Papa Haydn
> standing in his way, one more father to be defied or
> circumvented."

Or this one on Beethoven's relationship to Goethe, in the light of their meeting at Teplitz in 1812, after which Beethoven wrote, "Goethe delights far too much in the court atmosphere, far more than is becoming in a poet:" Tyson writes "In fact Beethoven's admiration for his fellow men usually flourished best at a distance." In all, this short account shows sensitivities to Beethoven's human weaknesses which remind us that Tyson had practiced psychoanalysis long before he turned to rigorous philological studies.

In Kerman's essay on the music, brevity is well compensated for by the prose and within the boundaries of a short article, quotable passages abound. Thus on the Opus 59 quartets: "All three quartet slow movements, surely, cry out for evocative titles, and the last two finales are all but orchestral in conception." Or on Opus 135:

> The last quartet, Op. 135 in F, is a brilliant study in Classical nostalgia, though it does not lack a vision of the abyss in the second movement and a characteristic response through hymnody in the third.

I turn now to Klaus Kropfinger's Beethoven article for the German encyclopedia, *MGG*, which is unusual in every respect. Kropfinger (1930–2016) edited works for the new Henle Beethoven edition, and he wrote on Beethoven and on aspects of contemporary music. His book on *Wagner and Beethoven* offered new perspectives on this supposedly well-worn topic, and his essays on twentieth-century music are consistently stimulating. This article on Beethoven, issued separately in paperback in 2001, goes even further than Kerman-Tyson beyond the usual boundaries of reference-book writing, and it may be the most original contribution of its kind in the modern Beethoven literature.

Kropfinger begins with a detailed chronological synopsis of the life, year by year, adding brief remarks along the way on a variety of personal topics – including Beethoven's family, friends, dwellings, compositions, sketches, finances, and much else. And at the end he includes a parallel annotated list of all of Beethoven's compositions, finished and unfinished, plus an extensive bibliography up to the year 2000. The main text of this compendium – for that is what it is – exceeds in interest almost any comparable reference source on Beethoven known to me, as he ranges over the field of research on Beethoven up to around 2000, often pointing out the limits of current knowledge, raising questions as he goes. This article is surely more easily grasped by experienced Beethovenians than by general readers. But it should be required reading for both.

Recent Biographies

As I come down now to recent contributions, I want to consider some of the larger trends in the background. Over the broad history of Beethoven biography and commentary we can distinguish different types of practitioners. One is made up of writers steeped in knowledge of Beethoven's life, his personal complexities and interactions, and the world in which he lived. These authors may also offer commentary on the music but put the claims of biography and history before those of close discussion of works, joining in the common and evidently well-justified belief that any such discussion is too technical for the common reader. Another, smaller group, consists of scholars who are devoted to what I will call the inner biography, the domain of Beethoven's creative life as it is documented by his many sketchbooks, composing scores, autographs, and related sources that can help to illuminate the stages of his compositional practice. This approach blends history and theory to some degree, and it belongs to the tradition that began with Nottebohm, who, as we saw earlier, actually defined his work as "biography," although it clearly moves along very different lines than those pursued by "normal" biographers. A third approach, which really lies outside history and biography, no matter how broadly we define them, is that of music analysis in the more rigorous sense.[23] It is a branch of study that grew in scope and in varieties of approach from about the mid-eighteenth century to the present, and for whom in modern times Heinrich Schenker became a central figure. The most rigorous practitioners of music analysis have tended to focus unswervingly on the works in all their structural qualities, avoiding discussion of the composer's life, career, or context. Not that such matters are not potentially of interest to music analysts, but that the nature of their work is such as to leave such matters to somebody else. In a useful introduction to the field of music analysis, the authors put it this way: "the main aim of the analyst is, through study, the enhanced understanding and enjoyment of particular compositions."[24] To practitioners with strong views of this kind, the works of Beethoven are structural embodiments of his thought and practice as seen within the domain of Western tonality, works that obviously emerged from his creative imagination but can be studied largely without reference to background and context.

Among Beethoven biographers prior to the mid-twentieth century, not many were much concerned with

---

[23] For a broad and richly informed summary of the history of analysis in Western music see Ian Bent, "Analysis," in *The New Grove Dictionary of Music and Musicians* (1st edn 1980) and subsequent editions.

[24] Jonathan Dunsby and Arnold Whittall, *Music Analysis in Theory and Practice* (New Haven: Yale University Press, 1988), 4.

music-theoretical sectors of knowledge and research, either
as a matter of personal training and outlook or because the
close analysis of works was not part of their intellectual mission. Thayer, who was a truly dedicated historian, devoted
years of effort to tracking down the documents that illuminate Beethoven's life and career. He was determined to set
the record straight, to correct the falsehoods and exaggera-
tions that had been broadcast by Schindler and others from
1840 onward. Thayer had a general background in music but
it is not clear that his musicality was highly developed, and
for his main pursuits it does not appear that it needed to
be. Such was the integrity of his research that after all the
revisions, additions, and updating that have taken place over
the 171 years since he began his work in 1849, his basic work
has stood the test of time.

The other specialists to whom I referred above, those
mainly interested in Beethoven's creative life, are open to a
broader biographical approach, as Nottebohm was, but do
not or cannot find room to do everything that might come
to hand. And the analysts, for whom the finished works, in
all their richness, are the essential subject, rarely show much
interest in the purely biographical issues, since for many of
them – and I do not mean this as a complaint – the vast
complexities of musical form and structure are all-encompassing. This traditional dichotomy, between biography and
analysis, between music history and theory – is of course
not limited to Beethoven – but with a composer as famous
and influential as Beethoven it is a highly visible feature
of the history of the field. Only in more recent times have
efforts to bridge the gap become visible.

In the remainder of this chapter I will comment briefly
on a selected group of recent Beethoven biographies, with
the exception of my own biography of 2003, which I will
discuss in the final chapter of this book at greater length.
By "recent" I refer to biographical works, closely or broadly
defined, that followed Solomon's *Beethoven* of 1977, one or
two of them having appeared in the 1990s before Solomon's

revised edition of 1998, but the majority after that year. My selected list, beginning with Solomon, is as follows:

Maynard Solomon, *Beethoven*, 1977; rev. edn 1998
Konrad Küster, *Beethoven*, 1994
William Kinderman, *Beethoven*, 1995; rev. edn 2009
David Wyn Jones, *The Life of Beethoven*, 1998
Barry Cooper, *Beethoven*, 2000
Lewis Lockwood, *Beethoven: The Music and the Life*, 2003
Elisabeth Brisson, *Beethoven*, 2004
Edmund Morris, *Beethoven: The Universal Composer*, 2005
Jan Caeyers, *Beethoven: Der einsame Revolutionär* (originally in Dutch), 2009; German edn 2012
Jan Swafford, *Beethoven: Anguish and Triumph*, 2014
John Clubbe, *Beethoven: The Relentless Revolutionary*, 2019
Mark Ferraguto, *Beethoven in 1806*, 2019

In what follows I will discuss the English-language works first, then those in German and French; my comments on my own biography will appear in Chapter 7.

William Kinderman

William Kinderman was trained as a pianist and his Beethoven scholarship is informed by his background in performance. Besides his teaching and contributions to scholarship Kinderman has also been a major organizer of conferences, and he was involved in the creation of the new Beethoven museum in Heiligenstadt, where the composer wrote the Testament in 1802. Alongside his publications on Beethoven and other composers Kinderman is also the general editor of a series of editions of the Beethoven sketchbooks.[25]

---

[25] Kinderman's series at the University of Illinois Press is a counterpart to the series initiated by the Beethoven-Haus in 1953. To date, three publications have appeared in the Illinois series; 1) the sketchbook MS Artaria 195, edited by Kinderman (2003);

His one-volume *Beethoven* came out in 1995 and again in a partially revised edition in 2009, somewhat parallel to the two editions of Solomon's biography of 1977 and 1998. As he wrote in the original preface, this book aims to elucidate the "main lines of Beethoven's creative development" and to incorporate new research. One of its special qualities among recent Beethoven books is its focus on aesthetic aspects of the music as seen in relation to the philosophical ideas that informed intellectual life in Beethoven's time. This especially means the writings of Kant and Schiller, but also of Friedrich Schelling, "a pivotal figure in the circle at Jena in the 1790s that included both Hölderlin and Hegel."[26] Its emphasis on the aesthetic background distinguishes Kinderman's book from almost all other biographical surveys of our time.

Much of the book offers cogent discussions of many works, moves through the changing periods of Beethoven's life, and explores areas little discussed elsewhere. Among them are Beethoven's vigorous sense of humor, mainly verbal but sometimes musical, so clearly a feature of his forthright way of grappling with the world around him. Kinderman's revisions in the second edition focus on particular works and topics, for example a comparison of Beethoven's Quintet for piano and winds, Op. 16, with Mozart's masterpiece for that combination, K. 452.[27] Other changes concern the *Eroica* Symphony, *Fidelio,* the piano sonatas Op. 106 and Op. 111, and the A-minor Quartet Op. 132. And the enlarged bibliography, covering Beethoven research and commentary up to 2009, further raised the quality of a valuable book.

---

2) the "Eroica" Sketchbook, edited by myself and Alan Gosman (2013); 3) the pocket sketchbook Grasnick 5, edited by Patrizia Metzler and Fred Stoltzfus (2016).

[26] William Kinderman, *Beethoven.* 2nd edn (Oxford: Oxford University Press, 2009), 7. The introductory pages of Kinderman's book make clear the importance of the contemporary philosophical background to his view of Beethoven.

[27] *Ibid.,* 48f.; and my *Beethoven: The Music and the Life,* 108.

Barry Cooper

Barry Cooper is among the most prolific Beethoven scholars currently active. He has taught for many years at the University of Manchester, and his publications on Beethoven include essays on a wide variety of topics but also an edition of the piano sonatas that is unusual in including the three early piano sonatas (WoO 47) that Beethoven wrote in 1783.[28] Another major undertaking was the handbook entitled *The Beethoven Compendium* (1991), of which Cooper was the principal editor, with contributions by Anne-Louise Coldicott, Nicholas Marston, and William Drabkin. This volume supplies a calendar of Beethoven's life, works, and relevant events, plus useful commentary on biographical topics, such as "Beethoven as an Individual," "Beethoven's Beliefs and Opinions," and much else.[29] To which we can add Cooper's books on *Beethoven and the Creative Process* (1990) and his *Beethoven's Folksong Settings: Chronology, Sources, Style* (1994).[30]

Though probably no single book on Beethoven, no matter what its length, can encompass the mass of facts, encounters, and events that belong to his biography and also do justice to the works, in all their genres, forms, and individuality – still, Cooper's one-volume *Beethoven* comes closer than most.[31] At the same time it shows a refreshing tendency towards skepticism about much that is received knowledge. As William Drabkin pointed out in a searching review, Cooper begins by reminding his readers that:

> surprisingly little is known for certain about Beethoven. Much is based on the accumulation of a weight of data

---

[28] On these sonatas see LvBWV, Vol. 2, 121–4 and Barry Cooper, *Beethoven*, (New York: Oxford University Press, 2000), 9–11.

[29] Cooper, *Beethoven Compendium*.

[30] 1) Oxford: Clarendon Press, 1990; and 2) same publisher, 1991.

[31] Barry Cooper, *Beethoven*.

that merely renders certain conclusions almost inescapable, others fairly probable, and others highly speculative or dubious though not impossible.[32]

His cautionary attitude is a healthy corrective to the frequent tendency of newcomers and generalists to simply repeat the formulas of the standard biographical portrait. To wit, his discussion of the problem of the "Immortal Beloved," which he singles out in his preface. As he writes, despite many conflicting attempts to identify the unnamed intended recipient of this famous letter of 1812:

> the evidence that she was Antonie Brentano is stronger than the evidence for many other widely held assumptions about Beethoven's life, yet it has been attacked vigorously in recent years by those who will not accept anything short of certain proof, which is unlikely to emerge.[33]

The book is richer in factual material than in discussions of the music, though both are ample, and Cooper tends towards a common-sense view of many problematic aspects of Beethoven's life and personality. These include Beethoven's notoriously difficult relationships to people around him – among them his patrons, his fellow musicians and composers, and his household servants. I believe most biographers would agree that, taking the evidence as we have it, in many aspects of his relation to the outer world Beethoven

---

[32] William Drabkin, review in *19th-Century Music*, XXVI (2002), 94–100; Cooper, *Beethoven*, x.

[33] *Ibid.*, In his detailed discussion of the problem (*Beethoven*, 207–212) Cooper reviews the evidence and the various candidates, and writes (210) "Solomon's case for Antonie...seems even more secure now than when it first appeared, for it has withstood vigorous attacks by several writers." Solomon had first presented the case in 1972 and repeated it in his *Beethoven* of 1977.

was estranged and difficult; that he was deeply wounded by
his deafness but perhaps also governed by a sense that if he
were to engage with the world in a more yielding manner it
might in some way limit or damage his commitment to his
artistic inner life and to his work. This attitude was always
present when he dealt with his servants. Consider this entry
from his *Tagebuch* of 1812–18:

> To live alone is like poison for you in your deaf condition;
> you always have to be suspicious with an inferior person
> around you.[34]

Solomon emphasized Beethoven's remoteness from many
people around him, and he cites a letter to Zmeskall of 23
July 1817 in which Beethoven says essentially the same thing
even more intensely: "...it drives me to despair to think that
owing to my poor hearing I am condemned to spend the
greater part of my life with *this* class of people, the most
infamous of all, and partly to depend upon them."[35]

In all, Cooper's book is ample, thorough, and useful as
a compendium on both the life and the works, without its
veering too strongly to one side or the other.

David Wyn Jones

The short biography by David Wyn Jones (1998) is a readable account of Beethoven's life and career, with minimal
commentary on the music. As William Drabkin said in a
review, Wyn Jones is especially good on historical context
and on the musical life in both Bonn and Vienna, on Beethoven's relationships to patrons and publishers, and on
the main stations of his life.[36] For a parallel, I think back to

---

[34] *Tagebuch* entry No. 137; see, among the publications of the
Tagebuch, Solomon's *Beethoven Essays*, 286.

[35] Solomon, *Ibid.*; *Briefe* No. 1143; Anderson No. 790.

[36] W. Drabkin, review of David Wyn Jones, *The Life of Beethoven*
(Cambridge: Cambridge University Press, 1998) in *The Musical*

Theodor Frimmel's brief biography of 1900, a comparison that illustrates advances in Beethoven scholarship in the past century. Wyn Jones is able to refer not only to Emily Anderson's English translation of the Beethoven letters (1961), as complete as she could then make it, but also to Sieghard Brandenburg's complete German edition, which had come out in 1996–98, just two years before Jones's book appeared. Jones's book shows wide knowledge of music and musicians of the era, as is evident also in his books on Haydn, on the symphony in Beethoven's Vienna, and other books on music and musical life in the classical period.

Other Recent Biographies

In closing, some brief comments on some other recent English-language biographical publications, by Edmund Morris (2005), Jan Swafford (2014), John Clubbe (2019) and Mark Ferraguto (2019).

Edmund Morris was not a music scholar but a professional biographer, the author of books on Theodore Roosevelt, Ronald Reagan, and Thomas Edison, noted for his stylish prose. Morris's book is essentially a personal appreciation of Beethoven by a music-lover, and in writing about the life he basically follows what I am calling the "standard model," in which the young hero is stricken with deafness but then finds the strength and resolve that carries him through to the great achievements of his later life. As Morris says in his acknowledgments he is strongly indebted to Thayer and Solomon, "both [of whom] revolutionized Beethoven scholarship," but he also cites a fair-sized array of other writings. His lively prose makes the book attractive to lay readers, and he begins and ends with anecdotes that reflect the power of Beethoven's music when heard in

Times (Summer 1999), 69–70. See also the review by Barry Cooper in _Music and Letters_, 80/4 (1999), 629–31.

difficult moments in modern life at which he was present. One was at Harvard during the blizzard of 1978, when amid disastrous weather conditions the Fifth Symphony finale rang out from a dormitory window; when the storm ended, "some of the listeners [were] crying." The other was at a New England summer concert in 2004, when a fire broke out at a nearby house. Firefighters arrived to put it out but did not interrupt the performance of the last quartet, Opus 135. As Morris puts it at the end of his book, "knowing that great music was being performed in the shed, they had come up the mountain without sirens, and were plying their hoses in silence."[37]

Jan Swafford

"Anguish and Triumph" is the subtitle of Jan Swafford's biography, and it foreshadows the flamboyant prose in which the narrative of the life is presented. As Edmund Morris pointed out in a review, much of the biographical presentation in this book is "relentlessly conversational, at times downright chatty," taking the known facts and situations as springboards for vividly described scenarios.[38]

The main text is a lengthy overview (more than 900 pages) of Beethoven's life and career, not without a few minor errors, such as the designation of the Archduke Rudolph as the Emperor Franz's "half-brother," when he was in fact his youngest brother.[39] It offers few new insights with regard to the life. But in compensation Swafford's book goes much further in discussion of the music than most biographers, although his comments are hard to find in the absence of

---

[37] Edmund Morris, *Beethoven: The Universal Composer,* (New York: Harper Collins, 2005), 1f., and 229.

[38] Edmund Morris, review of Swafford in the *Wall Street Journal,* 2 August 1914.

[39] Jan Swafford, *Beethoven: Anguish and Triumph,* (New York: Houghton Mifflin Harcourt, 2014), 516.

a separate list of even the major works and where to locate his observations about them in the main text. The book is really two books in one. The first is the main text, the other is in the endnotes, which often provide detailed comments on individual compositions and some interesting thoughts on broader issues.[40]

Among very recent books I can briefly mention two biographical contributions of different kinds. One is John Clubbe's recent book, *Beethoven: The Relentless Revolutionary* (2019). Focusing on the impact of revolution in the political world of Beethoven's time, above all the French revolution and its consequences, Clubbe gives us a kind of *roman à clef*, an overview slanted toward Beethoven "as a revolutionary not only in his music but also, and not least, in his social and political thinking."[41] Clubbe writes as a cultural historian, not a musicologist, and there are few musical insights to be found, but there are some elements in his depiction of the cultural background that will inform most readers.

Another very different contribution is Mark Ferraguto's book on the single year 1806 as a turning point in Beethoven's development. It is the year of the Fourth Piano Concerto, dedicated to Archduke Rudolph; and of the Opus 59 Quartets, which embody one of the great turning points in the history of this major genre. Also composed in 1806 was the Fourth Symphony, the revision of Leonore and the composition of its great Overture No. 3; the Violin Concerto; and the 32 Variations in C minor for piano, WoO 80. Ferraguto's focus shows the wide range of Beethoven's creative ambitions in this year and the vast range of styles and genres in

---

[40] The endnotes (running to almost one hundred pages) are unfortunately not included in the index.

[41] John Clubbe, *Beethoven: The Relentless Revolutionary*, (New York: W. W. Norton, 2019), xvii.

which he could then work his will in this highly productive year of what I like to call his "second maturity."

I come now to brief discussion of recent German and French contributions. Konrad Küster's short biography of 1994 is an intelligent and thoughtful book, mainly oriented towards the works but also raising interesting questions about the relationship of the works to the various stages of Beethoven's career. It is a book to which one can return for insights on particular compositions. The more recent book by Jan Caeyers is on a much larger scale, and shows the author's wide reading of the specialized literature, including Dieter Haberl's discovery that the young Beethoven's journey to Vienna in 1787 was much longer than had been formerly known.[42] Caeyers dwells at some length on some of the most poignant issues in Beethoven's life, including the "Immortal Beloved" question – to which he devotes several chapters. And he is up to date on recent discoveries, including Schindler's falsifications in the Conversation Books.

As to the French literature on the subject, the field has become more internationalized than it had been in the early twentieth century, when Romain Rolland could celebrate the glories of Beethoven as the hero who, "after a life of combat... from his tomb continued the fight for half a century in the kingdom of the spirit, where, high above our heads, our gods wage their eternal warfare."[43]

In 1955 there appeared a new Beethoven biography by Jean and Brigitte Massin, which showed in content and character that the older tendencies of French writers to glorify Beethoven rather than delve carefully and dispassionately

---

[42] Jan Caeyers, *Beethoven: Der einsame Revolutionär* (Munich: C. H. Beck, 2012), 85f. See my discussion of the year 1787 on pp. 146ff.

[43] Romain Rolland, *Beethoven the Creator*, Vol. 1, translated by Ernest Newman (New York: Garden City Publishing Co., 1927), 19.

into the historical and biographical framework of facts, had now come to an end. More recently, we can take note of the work of Elisabeth Brisson, who began with a finely calibrated study of Beethoven's knowledge of, and interest in, antiquity (2000), then published a short biography in 2004, and continued with a guide to Beethoven's music (2005).[44]

[44] Jean and Brigitte Massin, *Ludwig van Beethoven* (Paris: Club français du livre, 1955). Elisabeth Brisson, *Beethoven* (Paris: Fayard, 2004). Also valuable is her *Guide de la musique de Beethoven* (Paris: Fayard, 2005).

14. Maynard Solomon.

15. Joseph Kerman.

16. Alan Tyson.

17. William Kinderman.

18. Barry Cooper.

6
Exploring Beethoven's Life and Work: Three Sample Years

IN THIS CHAPTER I want to look again, now more narrowly, at the relationship of Beethoven's life and his work; how best to comprehend these two dimensions, which in some way we know must be two aspects of one. The focus here will be on three widely separated segments of his life: the years 1787, 1809, and 1826. Of course this problem in biography looks quite different in each of these periods, by virtue of Beethoven's age, his stage of development as man and musician, and all other relevant conditions.

A year in the life of a great artist can be a long time. This is especially true for one like Beethoven whose compositional styles changed so drastically across nearly five decades, from the earliest piano sonatas, written in his childhood, all the way to the late quartets. My hope is that narrowing the focus to three separate years may furnish insights that can be applied to his longer artistic career and its context. Comparable studies in literary biography are found in two books by the Shakespeare scholar James Shapiro – one on 1599 and its importance for Shakespeare's work, the other on 1606, the year of King Lear.[1] In Beethoven scholarship I pointed out earlier the value of studies that dig deep into shorter periods, in particular Martin Cooper's book on the last ten years and Mark Ferraguto on Beethoven in 1806. Studies like these

---

[1] James Shapiro, *A Year in the Life of William Shakespeare, 1599* (New York: Harper Collins, 2005); and idem, *The Year of Lear: Shakespeare in 1606* (New York: Simon and Schuster, 2015).

can be of value in something like the sense that analyses of
individual works can shed light on ways of thought that have
wider implications. They can bring us down to ground level
as we try to see how Beethoven's situation in a particular
year may have influenced the works he was producing at the
time. Further, research on what Beethoven did and wrote
in a single year may broaden modern understanding of the
factual landscape by bringing attention to details.

How outer and inner aspects of an artistic life relate to
one another is the underlying question of artistic biography. We might see them as frameworks superimposed on
one another, or as modes of experience that we feel must be
perpetually connected but are sometimes apart, sometimes
intertwined, like strands of a cable. Or they can be thought
of as being in an endless tension throughout the artist's life.
A negative way of looking at the problem was formulated by
Carl Dahlhaus, to which I referred in the preface to this book.
Going beyond the quotation I gave there, he continues:

> Scholarly exactitude, in biography on the one hand and
> analysis of the music on the other, leads to an almost
> insuperable separation of the two fields. It is a common-
> place, on the face of it, that a composer's biography needs
> to be written in order to shed light on his work, but it is
> ceasing to be self-evident.[2]

It goes without saying that my discussion of the following
short segments of Beethoven's life are only summaries of
what might be much longer studies – but those studies lie in
the future, if they are undertaken.

1787: The Young Beethoven's Journey to Vienna

As 1787 began, Beethoven had just turned sixteen. In June
of 1784, almost three years earlier at age thirteen, he had
been appointed court organist by the current Elector, the

---

[2] Dahlhaus, *Beethoven: Approaches to His Music*, 1.

Archduke Maximilian Franz. Obviously his talents were blossoming under the tutelage of his principal teacher, Christian Gottlob Neefe, and he was being noted as a local prodigy. He was the son and grandson of Bonn musicians, as his grandfather Ludwig (1712–73), originally from Mecheln in Flanders, had served as the Electoral Kapellmeister and was evidently a very skilled musician – his grandson in later years kept his portrait by him to the end of his life. His father, Johann van Beethoven (*c*. 1740–92) was a court singer at Bonn from the 1760s on, but by the time his son Ludwig was born in 1770 (the second of seven children), Johann was experiencing the gradual loss of his vocal abilities and showing other signs of growing instability. As young Ludwig entered his teen-age years, three of his siblings died very young, with the result that Johann's alcoholism and psychological decline put young Ludwig in the position of having to work to sustain his family just when he was beginning to dream of a successful musical career. A strong source of support was his mother, Maria Magdalena, about whom Ludwig was to write after her death, "she was such a kind, loving mother to me, my best friend."[3] As Solomon puts it, young Ludwig

> [grew up] in a home in which the son's natural role model, the father, had been toppled from his pedestal, the monumentalization of the grandfather took on heroic proportions, and this deeply affected Johann's attitude towards his oldest son, with, in turn, rich implications for the latter's course of development."[4]

By 1787 Ludwig was receiving acclaim as keyboard performer and budding composer, and in 1783 Neefe had published a notice praising him to the skies and taking special

---

[3] *Briefe*, No. 3; see Lockwood, *Beethoven: The Music and the Life*, 3–8.

[4] Solomon, *Beethoven* (1998), 21.

pride in having given him Bach's *Well-Tempered Clavier* to play and study. As Neefe had written: "This young genius deserves support to enable him to travel. He will certainly become another Wolfgang Amadeus Mozart if he continues as he has begun."[5] The reference to Mozart is telling. Everyone knew that the child Mozart had been the wonder of the age, welcomed at courts across Europe, regarded by seasoned observers as having "premature and almost supernatural talents."[6] The patrons at Bonn now hoped that they might be nurturing "another Mozart."

> Far away Vienna beckoned, as the musical center of central Europe and as the seat of the Habsburg imperial court. The connections between Vienna and Bonn were substantial. Elector Max Franz was a devoted Mozart admirer, and at one point it was rumored that he might bring Mozart to Bonn as his kapellmeister. Among the patrons in both cities not a few were Freemasons, as Mozart was, and some were also members of the Illuminati, an anti-clerical group that "exercised a powerful influence within the Masonic Lodges."[7]

Among the supporters of both Mozart and the young Beethoven was Count August von Hatzfeld, for whom Neefe, himself an Illuminist, wrote an obituary in 1787. Another was Count Ferdinand Waldstein, who came to Bonn in 1788 and became a Beethoven admirer.[8]

It was probably Max Franz who sponsored the young Beethoven's journey to Vienna in the early months of 1787, likely assuming that Beethoven might have lessons with

---

5   Cramer's *Magazin der Musik* for 2 March 1783; Cited and discussed by Thayer and many later biographers.
6   Charles Burney, *The Present State of Music in France and Italy* (London, 1771), cited by Solomon, *Mozart* (New York: Harper Collins, 1995), 3.
7   Solomon, *Mozart*, 323.
8   *Ibid.*, 326.

Mozart and make fruitful contacts there.[9] Whether Beethoven ever met Mozart we do not know, despite myths and stories, but the chances are that he would at least have called on Mozart or attempted to make contact.[10]

What is certain is that the young Beethoven was steeped in Mozart's music and was deeply influenced by him. Around 1790 we find a sketch leaf on which Beethoven wrote down a passage in C minor and wrote above it, "this passage has been stolen from Mozart;" and then he recomposes it and writes down these words: "Beethoven ipse" [by Beethoven himself"].[11] And in later years, despite all the changes in Beethoven's aesthetic outlook, Mozart remained a guiding image.[12] In December 1791, when Mozart died and the time had come for Beethoven to move to Vienna to study with Haydn, it was essentially in mourning for the loss of Mozart that Waldstein wrote in Beethoven's album, "By dint of unremitting effort you shall receive Mozart's spirit from Haydn's hands."[13]

Regarding Beethoven's journey to Vienna in 1787, new information came to light as recently as 2006. Up to then all Beethoven biographers had assumed that Beethoven's entire journey lasted about a month; that is, that he left Bonn about March 20, that he arrived in Vienna on April

---

[9] Ludwig Schiedermair, *Der junge Beethoven,* (Leipzig: Quelle & Meyer, 1925), 178.

[10] For a summary of the various claims about whether Beethoven may have met, played for Mozart, or heard Mozart play, see Clive, *Beethoven and His World*, 241f.

[11] On this passage and others of this kind, see my *Beethoven: The Music and the Life,* 55–62

[12] For a partial interpretation of this question see my "Beethoven before 1800: the Mozart Legacy," in *Beethoven Forum 3* (1994), 39–52; reprinted in M. Spitzer, ed., *Beethoven* (Farnham: Ashgate, 2015), 81–94.

[13] As translated in Clive, *Beethoven and His World*, 386.

7, stayed just shy of two weeks, and apparently left Vienna on April 20.[14]

But in 2006 Dieter Haberl revealed new evidence drawn from local records at Regensburg, in Bavaria, showing that on January 5, 1787, a certain "Hr. Bertenhoven, organist von Bonn," arrived by coach and that he stayed at the guest-house called the "Golden Spiegel."[15] Regensburg was on the main postal coach route from the Rhineland to Vienna. If Beethoven arrived there on January 5, he must have left Bonn on or before January 1, 1787, since postal-coach records show that the trip required at least 4½ days. Thereafter the evidence stops, but it is known that on 1 April Beethoven was in Munich, and later in April several records show him again in Bavaria. He was in Regensburg (24 April), in Munich (25 April) and in Augsburg (26 April). By then he was on his way back to Bonn, having received urgent news from his father of his mother's serious illness. Her death on July 17 was a shocking blow to him and to his family, already struggling

---

[14] For a summary of the known facts as they stood until Haberl's discoveries in 2006, see TF, 87; and Solomon, *Beethoven* 2nd edn, 40. An earlier basic contribution was that of Eduard Panzerbieter, "Beethoven's Erste Reise nach Wien im Jahre 1787," *Zeitschrift für Musikwissenschaft* 10 (1927/28), 153–161. So far as I know, the only recent Beethoven biographer who has taken note of this new dating of the journey is Jan Caeyers, *Beethoven: Der einsame Revolutionär* (Munich: C. H. Beck, 2012), 84f; I was also able to make reference to it in the German translation of my biography of 2003, with the title *Beethoven: Seine Musik, Sein Leben* (Kassel: Bärenreiter and Stuttgart, Weimar: Metzler, 2009), 29f.

[15] Dieter Haberl, "Beethovens erste Reise nach Wien. Die datierung seine Schülerreise zu W. A. Mozart," *Neues Musikwissenschaftliches Jahrbuch* 4 (2006), 215–55. See also Haberl's contribution to Christoph-Hellmut Mahling's *Musiker auf Reisen; Beiträge zum Kulturtransfer im 18. und 19. Jahrhundert* (Ausburg: Wißner-Verlag, 2011), 111ff.

for equilibrium owing to Johann's incapacities. A letter from the young Beethoven to his patron Joseph Wilhelm von Schaden in Augsburg (who had befriended him when he was there), speaks volumes about his deep pain over the loss of his mother, which was to have profound consequences for him throughout his life. He writes as well of his current physical ailments and his "melancholy, which for me is almost as great an evil as my illness itself."[16]

Accordingly, a new picture has begun to emerge about the young Beethoven's experience in the first months of 1787, and it is conceivable that his time in Bavaria could well have included contacts with important patrons there – but at present we know no further details. Perhaps more new documentation may be found that would enlighten us about his contacts on this journey. As to his work as composer in 1787, his talent, ambition, local encouragement, and probably his time in Vienna, had fired his dream of potential greatness. As he wrote to Neefe in 1792 or 1793, "If I become a great man, you will have a share in it..."[17] These words are revealing. At Bonn he had received lessons first from his father Johann (who for all his problems was a competent musician), then from Neefe and from a few other local musicians. Musical life at Bonn was on a very high level, thanks to Max Franz, and both opera and orchestral music were being intensively cultivated.[18]

---

[16] For the letter and discussion see my *Beethoven, the Music and the Life*, 3–8.

[17] *Briefe*, No. 6 (fragment). This excerpt was published by Neefe in the *Berliner Musikalische Zeitung*, No. 39, of 26 October 1793.

[18] Much new research on musical life at Bonn has been provided in recent years by Birgit Lodes, Elisabeth Reisinger, and John D. Wilson, including a complete reconstruction of the operatic library at the court and of musical life in the late 18th century. See *Beethoven und andere Hofmusiker seiner Generation*, edited by these three authors (Bonn: Beethoven-Haus, 2018; and

Beethoven's earliest surviving compositions were mainly
for keyboard, and as early as 1782 his Nine Variations on a
March by Ernst Christoph Dressler Variations in C Minor,
WoO 63, was published at Mannheim, with the young composer incorrectly cited as being ten years old – "agé de dix
ans".[19] And as for his other works of this time, new studies of
musical sources at Bonn have begun to alter accepted views
of when he may have composed a number of important early
works. Up to now it has been believed that between 1782
and 1787 Beethoven composed a number of works in diverse
genres. They include songs, such as WoO 107 and 108; keyboard sonatas (WoO 47); rondos for solo keyboard (WoO 48
and 49); a fugue for organ (WoO 31); a piano concerto (WoO
4); three piano quartets (WoO 36); a trio for piano, flute and
bassoon (WoO 37); a "Romance cantabile" for winds, piano,
and orchestra (WoO 207); and the first version of what was
to become his Second Piano Concerto, Op. 19 (with a different Rondo finale).[20] Very recently, however, new research by
John D. Wilson on the music manuscripts from this period
has cast doubt on the previously accepted dates of some
of these works, including the three piano quartets (WoO
36) and the piano concerto (WoO 4). The surviving score
of the piano quartets, evidently an autograph score, bears
the date "1785" and a note saying it was composed by "luis
van Beethoven/ agé 13" [corrected from "14"]." The birth-
year correction suggests that this heading could have been

The Operatic Library of Elector Maximilian Franz, ed. Elisabeth Reisinger, Juliane Riepe, and John D. Wilson in collaboration with Birgit Lodes (Bonn: Beethoven-Haus, 2018).

[19] This juvenile work was actually reprinted in 1803 by Hoff-
meister in Vienna, with a different musical text. See LvBWV,
Vol. 2, 152f. (WoO 63).

[20] For a convenient recent chronology see LvBWV, Vol. 2, 799ff.
For an extended study of Beethoven's early works and their
sources see Douglas Johnson, Beethoven's Early Sketches in the
"Fischhof Miscellany," 2 vols. (Ann Arbor: UMI, 1980).

added later, if it was written by Beethoven himself. Wilson has shown that paper used for the manuscript of WoO 36 "seems not to have arrived in Bonn until 1787 at the earliest," and that in other features the manuscript "most closely matches scores that be dated to 1788 or 1789."[21] Accordingly, the traditional dating of these important piano quartets to 1785 is now in doubt, and the chronology of Beethoven's early work in Bonn is now ripe for revision.

Yet even though some dates of composition are now in doubt, it remains that the larger repertoire of Beethoven's early works, before his move to Vienna in 1792 is a substantial collection. And the earlier portion of the "Kafka" miscellany of early Beethoven sketches, currently dated as beginning about 1786, gives us a window into the young composer's workshop as he began to bring his compositional talents to fruition. That many of them are for keyboard is not surprising.

The overt connections between his three piano quartets and two of Mozart violin sonatas of 1781 (K. 296 and K 379) are well known, and there is no need here to go over the details.[22] But what does hit home is the originality of these early chamber works, including Beethoven's use of the rare key of E♭ minor for the Allegro movement of No. 2. Equally telling is that a few years later he could lift themes and passages from these unpublished piano quartets and use them

---

[21] My quotations are from a private communication from Dr. Wilson, for which I am most grateful. A preliminary account of these redatings is found in his contributions to the volume *The Operatic Library of Elector Maximilian Franz*: 1) "The Collection's Genesis and Structure," co-authored with Elisabeth Reisinger, pp. 207–250; and "Catalogue Raisonné of the Surviving Operatic Sources," 254–450. Wilson will discuss this important new research as well in his "Music Papers in Electoral Bonn, 1770–1794," in *BBS* 13 (2018), forthcoming.

[22] For an extended discussion see my "Beethoven before 1800: The Mozart Legacy," *BF* 3 (1994), 47–50.

in his piano trio Op. 1 No. 3, and his piano sonatas of Opus 2. Of the trios of Op. 1, the first may be slightly earlier than Nos. 2 and 3, which date from 1794–95; they were first performed and published in 1795. As for the piano sonatas of Op. 2, they were also products of 1794–95 and first appeared in 1796.

We come back now to 1787 and young Beethoven's ten-week journey to Vienna and Bavaria. At sixteen he was undoubtedly looking to the future. But in mid-1787 he had to confront the tragedy of the loss of his mother, his father's chronic alcoholism, and the needs of his siblings. His experience of early loss coupled with dreams of future achievements was in sharp contrast, and left him, as I have put it elsewhere, "a virtual orphan at sixteen." And even though he continued to have support from his local patrons, he writes in his letter to von Schaden of his "very few happy hours" since his return from Vienna, his illnesses, his melancholy, and his want of money. As he puts it, "Fate is not favorable to me here in Bonn."

A little more than five years later he took the decisive step of moving to Vienna, to realize his dream of becoming a great composer in the same capital in which Mozart had lived and worked in his later years. But for the young Beethoven, the precarious balance between his continued growth as an artist and his limited ability to hold and maintain strong relationships with others around him, seems already to have become apparent, well before the deafness crisis that came upon him in the late 1790s.

1809: War; the Archduke Rudolph

In 1809 Beethoven was thirty-eight years old, by now the most acclaimed composer of his time. Despite his deafness, which had been increasing for more than ten years, he was fully active in composition and, as much as possible, at the piano. He was continuing to put on concerts, as well as he could, and in late December 1808, in a concert as memorable for its freezing weather as for its program, he had led the first performances of the Fifth and Sixth symphonies, the Fourth Piano Concerto with himself as soloist; the aria *Ah, Perfido;* an improvisatory Fantasia; two movements from the Mass in C; and his newly composed Choral Fantasy, with piano solo and orchestra.[23] It had taken place in the Theater-an-der-Wien, a venue given to him by the Vienna theater directors in recognition of his recent role in charity concerts.[24] Even so, Beethoven was angry at the theater directors for their delay in giving him a date for this concert, and the evening was marred by a breakdown during the Choral Fantasy. As he wrote to Breitkopf & Härtel on January 7, 1809:

> ...the musicians... were enraged that when, from sheer carelessness, a mistake had been made in the simplest and most straightforward passage in the world, I suddenly made them stop playing and called out in a loud voice, "Once more" – such a thing had never happened to them before...[25]

It was not the first time that Beethoven had had problems with performers we know from Ries, Spohr, and Joseph Röckel. Just a month earlier, either in rehearsals before a concert on November 15, 1808 or at the concert itself, there had been similar quarrels, according to an account recorded by Thayer.[26]

---

[23] Among many accounts of the concert, on 22 December 1808, see TF, 445–9; Barry Cooper, *Beethoven,* 179f. On 1809 as an important year for Beethoven see my "Beethoven's 'Harp' Quartet: The Sketches in Context," in William Kinderman, ed., *The String Quartets of Beethoven* (Urbana: University of Illinois Press, 2006), 89–108, especially 89–91.

[24] TF, 446.

[25] *Briefe,* No. 350

[26] TF, 446f.

Early in 1809 Beethoven's long-simmering dissatisfac-
tion with Vienna came to a head, despite all the support
he had received for years from his patrons, including Lichnowsky, Razumovsky, and Lobkowitz. In this same letter of
January 7, besides complaining bitterly about musical life
in Vienna, he reports his decision to accept an offer from
Napoleon's younger brother, Jerome Bonaparte, currently
installed as King of Westphalia, to "settle there [in Kassel]
as Kapellmeister at an annual salary of 600 gold ducats..."[27]
Whether he really meant to leave Vienna for this provincial
German setting may well be doubted, but in any case he
got his friends Ignaz von Gleichenstein and the Countess
Erdödy to intervene with some of his wealthiest patrons to
induce him to stay. And so, one month later, Princes Lobkowitz and Kinsky and Archduke Rudolph banded together
to guarantee him a lifetime annuity of 4000 florins as long
as he remained in the Austrian capital or in imperial lands.[28]
His own grandiose ideas for the contract show Beethoven
describing himself as an artist whose aim must be to
"achieve a position in which he can devote himself wholly to
the elaboration of great works and not be hindered by other
matters or economical considerations."[29] His pleasure over
this new assurance of financial security is clear in a letter to

[27] Anderson No. 192; *Briefe* No. 350. Jerome, as a younger brother
of Napoleon, had been set up in 1807 as king of this newly con-
figured domain in central Germany, with Kassel as its capital.
Jerome had already approached Beethoven in the fall of 1807,
after the departure of Johann Friedrich Reichardt, his first music director.

[28] For the contract and details, see TDR III, 125f.; TF, 455ff.;
and especially Martella Gutierrez-Denhoff, "'O unseeliges
Dekret': Beethovens Rente von Fürst Lobkowitz, Fürst Kin-
sky und Erzherzog Rudolph," in *Beethoven und Böhmen*, ed.
Sieghard Brandenburg and Martella Gutierrez-Denhoff (Bonn:
Beethoven-Haus, 1988), 91–145.

[29] TF, 456.

his friend Gleichenstein, to which he adds that "the title of Imperial Kapellmeister is to follow" and he encloses a copy of the annuity agreement. He writes,

> Now you can help me to look for a wife... but she must be beautiful, for it is impossible for me to love anything that is not beautiful; – or else I should have to love myself.[30]

It goes without saying that nothing came of the marriage idea, mingled as it is with yearning and ironic self-deprecation. The annuity gave him a welcome degree of financial stability, even if he had later problems in collecting it owing to Lobkowitz's insolvency and the Austrian currency devaluation in 1811, followed by Kinsky's sudden death in 1812. But this gesture of support, above all from Archduke Rudolph as a member of the royal family, was an important turning-point.

From now on, Beethoven, always conscious of his artistic stature, accepted his role as Rudolph's teacher, even though he later found as many reasons as he could to cancel lessons. Rudolph was a genuinely talented musician who understood what it meant to have Beethoven as his mentor.[31] Besides financial support, Rudolph gave Beethoven special favors, including access to his music library, and he made his subservience public with his *Forty Variations on a Theme by Beethoven* of 1818.[32] No one else in Beethoven's life comes close to Rudolph as both devoted patron and pupil, and Beethoven's feeling for this attachment is visible from then on in his letters and in the major works that he dedicated

---

[30] *Briefe*, No. 367; Anderson 202.

[31] For a thorough overview see Susan Kagan, *Archduke Rudolph, Beethoven's Patron, Pupil, and Friend* (Stuyvesant, NY: Pendragon Press, 1988).

[32] The work was published in a modern edition with commentary by Susan Kagan in the series *Recent Researches in the Music of the Nineteenth and Twentieth Centuries*, Vol. 21 (Madison: A-R Editions, 1992).

to Rudolph, above all the *Missa Solemnis,* but also many others, including the *Grosse Fuge.*[33]

In early May the war with France took a turn for the worse when Napoleon's battalions bombarded Vienna and occupied the city for more than six months.[34] Times were hard, life was disrupted. Yet such were the mixed views of the Viennese intelligentsia about current politics that the occupation was not seen by everyone as a total defeat but in some quarters felt like a temporary liberation from the censorship of the imperial regime. As Solomon describes Viennese life during these months,

> Napoleon's eagle perched on the masthead of the *Wiener Zeitung*; a cantata, *Sieg der Eintracht* was written by Ignaz Castelli and Joseph Weigl to celebrate the marriage of Napoleon to the Habsburg princess Marie Louise; the best artists of Vienna were called to Schönbrunn to perform for Bonaparte. Beethoven was not called.[35]

Beethoven's ambivalence towards Napoleon remained visible. On September 8 he conducted the *Eroica* at a charity concert, and in a private note to himself the following year Beethoven considered dedicating the *Mass in C* to Napoleon.[36] The French military occupation clearly disrupted his productivity, as he complained to Breitkopf on July 26:

[33] For insights into this important relationship, see Kagan, *Archduke Rudolph*; Birgit Lodes, *Das Gloria in Beethovens Missa Solemnis* (Tutzing: Schneider, 1977); Ronge, *Beethovens Lehrzeit*, 136ff; and my "Beethoven as Sir Davison," *BBS* 11 (2014), 133–140.

[34] Solomon, *Beethoven*, 2nd edn, 182 on the occupation and Beethoven's relationship to Napoleon.

[35] *Ibid.*

[36] See Hans Schmidt, "Die Beethoven Handschriften des Beethovenhauses in Bonn," *Beethoven Jahrbuch* 7 (1971), No. 494, dated 8 October 1810.

...since May 4 I have produced very little coherent work, at most a fragment here and there. The whole course of events has affected both body and soul... What a destructive, disorderly life I see and hear around me, nothing but drums, cannons, and human misery...[37]

His reference to the date of May 4 is telling, above all in a letter that he was writing three months later. May 4 was the date on which the royal family fled Vienna for Hungary, and the family included the Archduke. Rudolph's departure is directly linked to a major new work – the "Lebewohl" Sonata for piano Op. 81a. On the title page of the autograph manuscript Beethoven writes:

"Das Lebe wohl/ Wien am 4ten May 1809/ bei der Abreise S. Kaiserl. Hoheit/ des Verehrten Erzherzogs Rudolph."

("The Farewell/ Vienna on the 4th of May 1809/ on the departure of his Royal Highness the Honorable Archduke Rudolph").

Although Beethoven had apparently begun to sketch this sonata in April, he could well have known about the royal family's preparations for departure a few weeks before they left. And since the Archduke did not return until the end of January 1810, there was plenty of time during his absence for Beethoven to complete this sonata and to move on to other works. The personal significance of this sonata is its overt expression of Beethoven's relationship to Rudolph and the strength of emotion that the work embodies and reveals. This is visible from its very first measures, where Beethoven writes the word "Le-be-wohl" on the first three notes of the sonata, something he never did in any other of his instrumental compositions.[38] As Tovey noted, the

37 Anderson No. 220; *Briefe* No. 392.
38 On Op. 81a as an expression of his feelings, see Eytan Agmon, "Beethoven's Op. 81a and the Psychology of Loss," *Music Theory Online*, 2/4 (May 1996).

"Lebewohl" sonata "is a monument to the friendship of two men," a feeling that is reflected in other works he dedicated to Rudolph.[39] It is also his only truly programmatic piano sonata. It is a work about which he might have written, as he did for the Pastoral Symphony, "more the expression of feelings than tone-painting," but in which, nevertheless, a direct narrative of departure, absence, and return explicitly governs the emotional landscape of the three movements, as their titles indicate. Beethoven went to great pains to get his publishers to get these titles right, and when they first sent him proofs of the sonata with French titles for the movements but not German, he set them straight. He writes:

> [1]: "make the title read as I wrote it, in French and German, not in French alone" (letter to Breitkopf of 20 May 1811); and [2] in his letter to Breitkopf of 9 October 1811: "I have just received the "Lebewohl"... [and] I see that you have published other c[opies] with a French title [page]. Why, pray? 'Lebewohl' means something very different from 'Les Adieux.' The former is said in a warm-hearted way to one person; the other to a whole assembly, to whole towns..."[40]

[39] Donald Francis Tovey, *A Companion to Beethoven's Pianoforte Sonatas* (London: Associated Board of the Royal Schools of Music, 1931), 188. Other works dedicated to Rudolph are the Fourth Piano Concerto; the G-Major Violin Sonata, Op. 96; the Bb-Major Piano Trio, Op. 97 (forever known as "the Archduke"); the "Hammerklavier" Sonata, Op. 106; the Piano Sonata, Op. 111; the *Grosse Fuge* for string quartet, when it was published separately as Op. 133; and the four-hand arrangement of it that Beethoven made as his Op. 134; and, of course, the largest of all his sacred works, the *Missa Solemnis*, intended for Rudolph's installation as Archbishop of Olmütz in 1819.

[40] For the letter of 20 May see *Briefe* No. 499; for that of 9 October see *Briefe* No. 523. In a note to this letter (No. 523, n. 9) Sieghard Brandenburg correctly points to the contemporary

"In a warm-hearted way to one person" – this sums up his feeling that this work is his personal artistic gift to his young patron, the royal Archduke who is now to give him financial support for the future and also be his devoted pupil.

Beethoven's productivity is visible in his main sketch-book for 1809, which has been published in full in a critical edition.[41] During the year he completed a series of highly diverse and significant works. They include the Fifth Piano Concerto, Op. 73; the "Lebewohl" sonata; the String Quartet Op. 74; a number of songs; the piano Variations, Op. 76; the Fantasie for piano, Op. 77; the F♯-major piano sonata Op. 78; and the G-major sonatina Op. 79. To which he added some patriotic military marches and his first ideas for what became the "Namensfeier" Overture, now sketched in E♭ but later converted to C major when he came back to it seven years later. And as a patriotic gesture in this turbulent year he also sketched a military anthem on the text "Österreich über alles," on a text by Heinrich von Collin.[42]

We saw that Beethoven wrote in July that since May 4 he had written "very little coherent work, at most a fragment here and there." Whether this was literally true we can't be sure, but quite possibly his productivity was hampered by living under military siege and invasion. If so, he regained momentum in the ensuing months. But still, the war took its toll. In November he tells Breitkopf that "We are enjoying a little peace after violent destruction, after suffering every hardship that one could conceivably endure..." and at the end he adds, "What do you say to this *dead peace* [the peace

---

genres of works that were "farewells" to certain cities, such as *Les Adieux de Paris* or *Les Adieux de Londres*.

[41] *Ludwig van Beethoven: Ein Skizzen Buch aus dem Jahre 1809 (Landsberg 5)*, ed. Clemens Brenneis 2 vols. (Bonn: Beethoven-Haus, 1993).

[42] For the military song sketches see LvBWV, Vol. 2, 602f., Unv. 18, with valuable commentary.

treaty signed in October 1809]? I no longer expect to see any stability in this age. The only certainty we can rely on is *blind chance*."[43]

In all, 1809 was a hard year for him and for everyone in Vienna – and yet he was able to sustain his productivity at a remarkably high level as he produced a series of major works. We get the sense that he was finding new ways to effectively protect his inner creative life from the clashes and struggles of the world around him. There may be a lesson for his biography that can be drawn from 1809, the one year of his life in which Beethoven was literally exposed to war, bombardment, invasion, and a feeling of external danger, yet was able to respond by creating a personal shell of resistance to outside events that enabled him to continue to produce and grow as an artist.

1826: The Final Phase; the Late Quartets; Karl's Attempted Suicide; the Last Months

If we take the year 1826 as a whole and look back from the year's end to all that had passed, what Beethoven accomplished in this last calendar year of his life testifies once more to his immense strength of purpose. In the early months of the year his ongoing health problems had worsened, and in the summer his long-suffering nephew Karl, in despair, had reached a major crisis that resulted in his suicide attempt. By December Beethoven's intestinal problems became exacerbated by fever, chills, and inflammation of the lungs, and now premonitions of death were in the air. Over the last months before his death on March 26, 1827, he was visited by old friends and acquaintances who wanted to see him for the last time.

---

[43] Letter of November 22; *Briefe* No. 408; Anderson No. 228.

How Beethoven in 1826 was able to protect the inner world of his musical imagination from the emotional maelstrom of his outer life and complete two works as deep, complex, and different from each other as his string quartets Opus 131 and Opus 135, remains forever inexplicable. It feels as if his removal of his creative persona to a place of safety from the disorder of his outer life must have been even more decisive than in the past, not only because of his failing health and his nephew obsession, but because these works reach into hitherto unknown aesthetic territories. "Each in its own way," as Beethoven was reported to have said about his late quartets to Karl Holz, who reported it years later to Wilhelm von Lenz.

The C♯-minor quartet, Opus 131, remains one of his most conceptually difficult works, so deeply integrated in its structure and in the relationship of its diverse movements that it took many decades to be accepted by even the most astute commentators.[44] And as for Opus 135, with its return to the smaller proportions of an earlier classical era, its subtleties are concealed within a more accessible, familiar, and even humorous framework. It presents aspects of Beethoven's late style in a kind of classicizing disguise. The same is true for the "little" finale for Opus 130, the last complete movement that he was able to finish, late in 1826.

For the past few years Beethoven had been almost completely enveloped in work on his last quartets, the first three of which had been commissioned by Prince Nikolaus Galitzin in November 1822. These were his Opus 127 (composed between May 1824 and January 1825); Opus 132 (January–July 1825); and Opus 130 with the *Grosse Fuge* as its finale (*c.* May–December 1825). Soon thereafter he agreed to separate

---

[44] A recent study of the reception of Opus 131 is that of Megan Ross, *The Critical and Artistic Reception of Beethoven's String Quartet in C♯ Minor, Op. 131* (Ph.D diss., University of North Carolina, 2019).

the fugue from Opus 130 and publish it as an independent composition, and so it became Opus 133.

It was directly after the *Grosse Fuge* that he began work on the C#-minor quartet Opus 131 – which must have needed all his concentration until he finished it in July. It is doubly interesting to see that the monumental and innovative *Grosse Fuge* is followed by the fugal Adagio first movement that opens Op. 131, as different in character from the *Grosse Fuge* as can be imagined but with something like the same profound expressivity and complexity. Opus 131 was finished by August, as we know from correspondence and conversations. And somehow, between July and December, despite worsening health and the personal catastrophe of Karl's attempted suicide in early August, he was able to make a four-hands keyboard arrangement of the *Grosse Fuge* and to compose the F-major quartet, Opus 135. And even after that he was able to produce the "little" finale for Opus 130 as replacement for the *Grosse Fuge*. Then, in late November, his energy failing, he wrote down some ideas for a string quintet in C major, WoO 62, but could not bring it anywhere close to completion.[45]

Throughout 1826, the most painful difficulty in his outer life lay with Karl. For years Beethoven had struggled to obtain his nephew's guardianship, after the death of his brother Caspar Carl in 1815, battling incessantly to take Karl away from his mother, Johanna. The Beethoven literature is rife with commentary on Beethoven's psychological state both during and after his legal victory, as he sought to make Karl his "son," as he called him more than once. However he tried, Beethoven could never balance his own emotional needs with those of his beleaguered young nephew, who did all he could to accommodate the demands of his deaf

---

[45] The most recent discussion of the unfinished quintet is by Sabine Kurth, *Beethovens Streichquintette* (Munich: W. Fink Verlag, 1995), 277–88.

and overbearing uncle but could never find a true modus vivendi.[46]

We have no ready answers to the questions raised by even the most superficial account of Beethoven's life in 1826 and what he accomplished in that year. After Karl was released from the hospital in September, Beethoven took him to recuperate at his brother Johann's country estate at Gneixendorf. And there too the reports and anecdotes show Beethoven's immersion in his inner life. Thus the story of brother Johann's cook trying to make Beethoven's bed while he "sat at a table gesticulating with his hands, beating time with his feet, muttering and singing."[47] Or the tales told later by two peasants who remembered seeing Beethoven in the fields, whom they "took for a madman and kept out of his way." And we have the report of a young farmer who was driving a pair of oxen "when he met Beethoven shouting and waving his arms about in wild gesticulation," frightening the cattle, oblivious to his surroundings.[48]

And then, in the last weeks of 1826, after his return to Vienna in the first days of December, his increasing physical decline and, on March 26, 1827, his death. Three days later, thousands of Viennese joined the funeral procession for which Franz Grillparzer wrote the oration that set the long history of Beethoven biography in motion.

---

[46] See Solomon, "Beethoven and His Nephew" in Solomon's *Beethoven Essays* and his *Beethoven*, 2nd edn, 297–330.

[47] TF, 1007.

[48] *Ibid.*

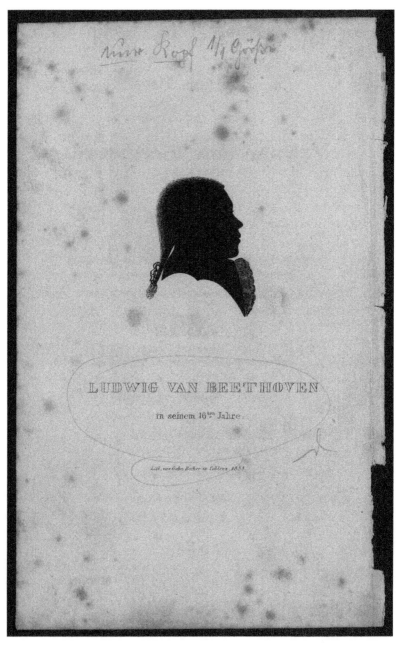

19. Beethoven as a Youth: Lithograph by the Becker Brothers of a
Joseph Neesen silhouette of Ludwig van Beethoven, age 15.

20. Beethoven in Middle Age:
Drawing by Ludwig Ferdinand Schnorr von Carolsfeld, 1810.

Ludwig van Beethoven

21. Beethoven in Old Age:
Lithograph from a drawing by Johann Stephan Decker, 1824.

7

Reminiscences and Reflections

In closing, I will offer some further thoughts on artistic biography and some reflections on my own contribution to it in my book *Beethoven: The Music and the Life* (2003).[1] A biography in our time can't be just a new report of the known facts. To be of value it needs a premise that informs the narrative and controls the interpretation. Such a premise may be focused on different aspects of the subject. It may center mainly on the works themselves and on the subject's development as an artist; or on what can be known of the subject's personality and relationships, close and distant; or on his or her political or spiritual outlook and world-view. It may touch on all of these and other topics, with a binding focus on a few of them. But in the modern age a purely factual biography, narrowly construed as a step-by-step account of the particulars of the life, no matter how comprehensive, may not be strong enough to create the profile that the genre demands and that readers need and want. The biographer needs to have the facts securely in hand but also needs to try to unearth their meanings and suggest their implications. And he surely needs to deal with some aspects of the works themselves, which for many readers is the raison d'être of the whole enterprise.

---

[1] New York: W. W. Norton, 2003; paperback edn, 2005. In this chapter I am drawing upon, and expanding some material from my essay, "Reappraising Beethoven Biography," published in the *Yearbook of Comparative and General Literature*, 53 (2007), 83–100.

The abiding problem of artistic biography – how to do justice to the life and to the works and how to relate the two dimensions – was the question I felt most keenly in writing my own biography of Beethoven. I tried to deal with it first by acknowledging how hard it is to handle and by noting its pervasive presence in all artistic biography, whether or not it is explicit. To widen my view I read or re-read a number of biographies of writers, artists, and scientists. Among them are those of Abraham Pais on Einstein, of Nicholas Boyle on Goethe, and of Richard Holmes on Coleridge and Shelley.[2]

For many musicians, when it comes to the biographies of great composers, pessimism reigns – as in the remarks I quoted earlier by Donald Francis Tovey and Carl Dahlhaus. It is, after all, a familiar experience that people deeply interested in music as structure or expression are often unable to see how knowing a great deal about a composer's life can advance their understanding of the works. In literature a heated reaction of this kind was voiced by Colin Burrow in a review of a biography of John Donne:

> literary biography is one of the background noises of our age... like the Sunday papers or chatter on a train. It gives the punters a bit of history and a bit of literature, and perhaps a bit of gossip, and... it saves them the trouble of reading history. And poems, too, for that matter... even the best examples can't entirely avoid the naive reduction of literature to evidence or symptom – epiphenomena

---

[2]   A. Pais, *Subtle is the Lord: The Science and the Life of Albert Einstein* (Oxford: Oxford University Press, 1982); N. Boyle, *Goethe: The Poet and the Age*, 2 vols. to date (Oxford: Oxford University Press, 1992, 2000); R. Holmes, *Shelley: The Pursuit* (London: Weidenfeld and Nicolson, 1974); Idem, *Coleridge: Early Visions* (New York: Viking, 1990); Idem, *Coleridge: Darker Reflections* (London: Harper Collins, 1998).

which are brought about by, and are potentially reducible to, biographical origins.[3]

Yet even though a close factual narrative may seem at times to be irrelevant to the artist's work and even though we struggle to fill in the biographical portrait, apply it to the work, and often come up short in the process – still we have to admit that in the final analysis the divided selves we are looking at belong to one person, whose character and actions combine to form a persona that the artist himself or herself helped to create for us – what Elisabeth Young-Bruehl calls the artist's "creative character."[4] She puts it this way:

> Creative people... create whatever they create in the medium of, through the developmental lineaments and structures of, their characters. They have... an image of their characters, or, in other terms, of their general psychic (mind and body) organization, which they both aspire to – it is an idealized image – and project into whatever they create... Creators are their own border guards, charged with stamping their cipher – their psychic 'character' in the graphic sense – on all departing products of their minds.[5]

Works of art do not materialize out of time and space. They are made by men and women who are born and raised in particular circumstances and who live in the world as they find it. They are partly shaped by, and react to, the social, political, and cultural conditions of their times as well as the traditions they inherit, traditions they feel compelled first to master and then to overcome. What they were trying to do and how they did it is vital in what we mean by biography.

---

[3] Review of J. Stubbs, *Donne: The Reformed Soul*, in *London Review of Books*, 28 (2006), 4.

[4] Elisabeth Young-Bruehl, *Creative Characters* (New York: Routledge, 1991).

[5] *Ibid.*, x.

One way out of the impasse, I suggested in my own book, is to try out the idea that for the biographer the subject's life and work are not independent categories, but that nevertheless they can't be treated as if there were no important differences between them. I suggested that it might be possible to separate what we see as the artist's "life" – as a story of personal events, experiences, and encounters of every kind – from his or her "career," that is, the part of the life that the artist devotes squarely and directly to the making and promotion of the works. Elusive and difficult as it may be to make such a distinction, for an artist like Beethoven I believe it can be of help. Focusing on his career helps us understand the lifetime importance of his craft and art as a pianist, performer and improviser but also as organizer and conductor of concerts; how he struggled financially without a fixed position; how he dealt with his patrons as vital sources of support but whose social pretensions he mainly despised; why so many of his letters are addressed to his publishers, with frequent complaints about their incompetence, a subject on which he remained fixated to the end of his life.

Thinking about his career and his need to promote it helps us understand his dealings with friends, associates, performers, and patrons, all of whom he used, sometimes shamelessly, to further his position in the world. It's true that as a free-lance composer without a secure paid position he had little choice, but his fierce independence was also linked to his stormy personality, noted by all his contemporaries. It emerged from his all-encompassing sense of self, his inner drive to be a wholly committed artist, conscious of his place in history, gaining and holding his position at the forefront of the musical world of his time. In part this fundamental commitment helps us understand his inability to form a lasting relationship with a woman. That he was well aware of this painful condition is not just a matter of speculation. In a conversation book of 1823 he reminisces about his early affair in 1800 with Giulietta Guicciardi, who had gone off to Italy with her husband, Count Wenzel Robert Gallenberg. Now, two decades later, the couple had returned to Vienna, and thus the conversation about them. Beethoven, writing in the conversation book, says that "she loved me more than she ever loved her husband..." and then he continues, "she sought me weeping, but I rejected her... if I had wanted to give my life's strength to such a life, what would have remained for the noble and better things?"[6]

This powerful sense of self resonates with his relationship to Napoleon, incomparably the contemporary example of the individual who rose from nothing to become the conqueror of Europe. Everyone knows that the young Beethoven admired Napoleon as general and as First Consul, then tore up the dedication of the Third Symphony when Napoleon declared himself Emperor. Instead of naming the symphony "Bonaparte," his original plan, he changed its title to "Heroic Symphony," a work written "to celebrate the memory of a great man," with its Funeral March embodying the elegiac and commemorative aspects of heroism. By inserting death into the heroic, Beethoven made what would have been primarily a powerful work into one of epic character. It became a major turning point of his artistic development.

We get further glimpses of Beethoven's self-consciousness in his largest works – those intended not only for contemporary audiences but for the future and the world at large – the *Missa Solemnis* and the Ninth Symphony among them. We see it also in his writings, as in a letter he wrote to the Archduke Rudolph, in March 1819. First he congratulates the prince on becoming an Archbishop and he thinks ahead to the great Mass that he intends to write

---

6   Beethoven, *Ludwig van Beethovens Konversationshefte*, (Leipzig: VEB Deutscher Verlag für Musik, 1976), Vol. 2, 365–7. Earlier quoted by B. Cooper, *Beethoven*, 110, among others.

for Rudolph's installation. But then he tells his royal pupil
who is the real master between them:

> Your... command that I should come, and indeed your
> intimation that [you] would let me know when I should
> do so, I was never able to fathom, for I never was, still am
> not, and never will be, a courtier.[7]

In this same letter he conjures up the image of an artist-ruler,
his imagined Rudolph of the future – but who is also himself – when he writes:

> Your Imperial Highness [as Archbishop and as com-
> poser] can create in two ways – both for the happiness of
> very many people and also for yourself. For in the present
> world of monarchs, creators of music and benefactors of
> humanity have been lacking up to now.

And in another letter, one of the most revealing he ever wrote,
Beethoven says that "in the world of art, as in the whole of
creation, freedom and progress are the main objectives."[8]

With such considerations in mind, I tried in my own
biography to center on Beethoven the composer. I focused
mainly on his artistic development from early to late, while
trying to do justice, but more succinctly, to Beethoven the
man. Thus my subtitle, "The Music and the Life," which I
consciously borrowed from Abraham Pais's biography of
Albert Einstein, to which I referred earlier. Pais's book is an
unsparing scientific exegesis in which many aspects of the
life are dealt with but in brief, sometimes laconic, terms,
while Einstein's early work in relation to the earlier state of
theory and knowledge in physics, the restless intellectual
and visionary concentration that underlay his great discoveries, spreads constantly into the foreground. With Pais you

---

[7] Letter of 3 March 1819; *Briefe* No. 1292; Anderson No. 948. See
     my *Beethoven: The Music and the Life*, 374.

[8] Letter of 29 July 1819; *Briefe* 1318; Anderson No. 955.

not only get a description of black-box radiation and early quantum theory, you also get the equations.

What I wanted was to maintain a balance between the claims of biography and those of critical understanding of the music, but with a bias towards the music. And since in a book of reasonable length I had to say something about nearly every work that Beethoven wrote, the resulting product turned out to have a greater emphasis on the music than on the details of the life, although I do not think that there is any truly important issue in Beethoven's life that is not discussed, at least briefly.

At the same time I had to pass over some works much more quickly than I would have liked, and I confess that there are a few works of special interest, such as the Quintet Op. 29, that were entirely neglected. I also see now that my focus on the political context of the period, including above all the continuing warfare between France and the various coalitions that opposed it, first in the post-revolutionary years and then under Napoleon, came at something of a cost to the portrait of the contemporary social systems, hierarchies, and personalities that directly impinged on Beethoven's life. More than one comprehensive study remains to be written about the relationship between Beethoven's achievements and the social and cultural transformations that were taking place in his lifetime, only some of which have yet been discussed by historians.

In closing, I want to consider another essay by Elisabeth Young-Bruehl, entitled "The Writing of Biography," that this astute biographer published in 1983 in the *Partisan Review* and later included in her book, *Mind and the Body Politic*.[9] I have yet to read a more incisive discussion

---

[9] *Partisan Review*, 1983; New York: Routledge, 1989. At the time of writing this essay and her biography of Anna Freud (1988), Young-Bruehl was not yet a psychoanalyst, as pointed out to me by Ava Penman.

of some of the primary issues in biography, and I strongly recommend it even though I want to take issue with some of its premises. One of Young-Bruehl's strategies is to set up as a universal problem the temptation to capture what she calls "the essence of a life," a temptation that she finds to be widespread and that, as she says, "takes nourishment from the psychological milieu." She sees how deep the impulse is in biographers to try to achieve this goal but she is determined to resist it, and she does so with illustrations that show how biographers have sought to bring it off and how, in her view, they have failed. She spells out four forms of the "temptation." The first is when a biographer looks for the "ruling intellectual universal, the key question, the object of your subject's intellectual quest," and then the biographer tries to show the life and work in harmony. The second arises when biographers select from the subject's traits of character "those that harmonize beautifully or clash intriguingly," to bring off a "vivid, lifelike" portrayal. In a third form, the biographer looks for an "event or series of events that seems to epitomize the subject's entire life" – thus representing the life as having a major turning point, a *peripateia*, that was crucially important and "after which – or during which – everything changed." And the fourth approach shows the subject "as a part standing for the whole, a symbol, a rallying point [...] You capture the subject poised like Liberty leading the people, Justice holding her scales. Biographical portraiture of this sort resembles panoramic painting." She takes as examples Ernst Cassirer's biography of Kant, and the work and comments of other writers, from Virginia Woolf and Lytton Strachey to Jean-Paul Sartre's biography of Jean Genet, and her own biography of Hannah Arendt. At the time of writing this essay Young-Bruehl had not yet written her biography of Anna Freud, published in 1988. Later Young-Bruehl turned to feminism and psychoanalysis in her *Subject to Biography*, 1998.

With full recognition of the subtlety that Young-Bruehl brought to her arguments, when it comes to artistic biography I have to take issue with her on one basic point. For with truly great artists, whether Beethoven, Shakespeare, Michelangelo, or others, the pull towards essentialism in biography is not, in my view, a limitation but rather is virtually inevitable. It follows from the fact that all we know about major artists, past and present, tells us that they define their lives as being primarily conditioned by the riveting obsession to produce the works they feel to be the raison-d'être of their being in the world. Every major artist of whom we have even approximate knowledge has recognized such an obsessive drive to creation as the motor force that gives meaning to their lives. In some instances that give us insight into artists' awareness of their creative drive and its importance, we also see an insatiable curiosity about their own art-world. Mozart once described himself as being "soaked in music," and, as his early biographer Niemetschek reports, he once told a fellow musician in Prague that

> people are mistaken if they think that my art has come easy to me. I assure you, my dear friend, no one has devoted so much effort to the study of composition as I have done. There is scarcely a famous master in music whose works I have not diligently, and often repeatedly, studied.[10]

Even the best Mozart biographies of our time have not done full justice to this aspect of Mozart's life, namely his close and deep study of exactly what he derived from the music of Bach and Handel, who were certainly among his main models in his last years, and the Italian and Italianate

---

[10] Franz Niemetschek, *Life of Mozart (Lebens des K. K. Kapellmeisters Wolfgang Gottlieb Mozart,* 1798). Translated by Helen Mautner, (London: Leonard Hyman, 1956), cited by Robert Marshall, ed., *Mozart Speaks: Views on Music, Musicians, and the World.* (New York: Schirmer Books, 1991), 200.

composers whose works he knew. This is not the Mozart of Peter Schaffer's *Amadeus*, a rakish person gifted with God-like powers. It is the real Mozart.

By supporting a biographical focus on the artist's work I do not mean that this is the only fruitful approach, but I do mean that in writing an artist's biography we do not have to worry as much about getting a reasonable balance between life and works, because most of them never had anything like a reasonable balance – the life was weighted heavily, in some cases absolutely, towards what Yeats called "the per-fection of the work." For artists on this level this is not what we might call a matter of choice; the artist feels that it is thrust upon him. Thus Rainer Maria Rilke, who as a young man knew Tolstoy and also served as secretary to Rodin in Paris, said of the great writer and the great sculptor that their lives apart from their work "seemed almost to wither away, like some organ they no longer require."[11]

It is possible to write the life of such a person without putting the work in the foreground, or simply intertwining it into the narrative of events and encounters, but to my mind it is inevitably unsatisfying. Recognition of the deeply rooted function of artistic work in the life, and therefore knowledge of the work and its contexts, professional competence in how to talk about it, and some acceptance of biographical essentialism, seem to me required for credibility in the work of a serious biographer.

Future Prospects

What might future Beethoven biographers seek to accom-plish in new ways? One task will be to come to grips in full detail with the world of music and musicians around Beet-hoven, the world he knew and that knew him. We have many first-hand personal accounts by contemporaries, including

---

[11]   See my *Beethoven: The Music and the Life*, 18 and 493 n. 24.

his visitors and others whose conversations were preserved in the conversation books – but we have very little by way of synthesis from this point of view. Few composers dominated their times as thoroughly as he did, but precisely for that reason there is an urgent need to bring his contemporaries out of the shadows. I would include in this list the greater and lesser composers of opera – including Rossini, about whom much has been written of late – but also Weber, Paer, and Cherubini, and the other composers of French, German, and Italian opera in these post-revolutionary and early Romantic years. The same is true for the contemporary composers of instrumental music, many of them performers – and for them a good beginning has been made by David Wyn Jones in his study of composers of symphonies in Beethoven's time.[12]

At a more general level, showing how critics in his time responded to Beethoven and his music, we now have conveniently available the large body of contemporary reviews of his works, both as published and as performed in concerts in his lifetime, compiled by Stefan Kunze.[13] And full English translations of the great mass of this critical material, in German, from Beethoven's lifetime, made by Robin Wallace, are now also available, first in two published volumes up through Beethoven's opera *Fidelio*, Opus 72; and the remainder, from there on to the last works, is now available on the website of the Boston University Center for Beethoven Research.[14]

---

[12] David Wyn Jones, *The Symphony in Beethoven's Vienna* (Cambridge: Cambridge University Press, 2012).

[13] Stefan Kunze, *Ludwig van Beethoven, Die Werke im Spiegel seiner Zeit* (Laaber: Laaber-Verlag, 1987).

[14] The published volumes are *The Critical Reception of Beethoven's Compositions by his German Contemporaries*, ed. Wayne M. Senner, Robin Wallace and William Meredith (University of Nebraska Press, 1999 and 2001).

Years ago Wallace provided a fine introduction to this whole subject.[15]

My list would also include the major performers of his time, singers and instrumentalists. Foremost among the latter would be the great French violinists, such as Kreutzer, Baillot, and Rode (all of whom knew Beethoven), and of course Ignaz Schuppanzigh and Franz Clement. And we should add the French cellist Jean Louis Duport, for whom Beethoven wrote the Op. 5 sonatas in Berlin, but also the Krafts (Anton and Nikolaus) and Joseph Linke. It would include the important pianist-composers, from Clementi to Tomaschek, Dussek, and Hummel, and the fifty composers who wrote single variations on Diabelli's waltz for the "other" volume that Diabelli published in 1824. It would re-examine Schubert's extraordinary achievements in the light of his complex relationship to Beethoven. And it would have ample room for the Archduke Rudolph, who has to be reckoned as a competent composer whose works for chamber ensemble deserve to be better known (Susan Kagan has given us a very good start).[16] Closer study of the contemporaries should be carried out in the context of the larger social and cultural developments in Austria and Europe between 1789 and 1830, when massive change was taking place as the Napoleonic wars were fought and won, and as the industrial revolution was reshaping European economic and political life.

Despite the growth of Beethoven scholarship and research over the past half-century, and its increasingly international character, many important tasks remain. The most basic is the completion of the critical edition of Beethoven's works, as published by Henle Verlag, which still has

[15] Robin Wallace, *Beethoven's Critics: Aesthetic Dilemmas and resolutions during the composer's lifetime* (Cambridge: Cambridge University Press, 1986).

[16] Susan Kagan, *Archduke Rudolph, Beethoven's Patron, Pupil, and Friend* (Stuyvesant: Pendragon Press, 1988).

a fair distance to go despite the valiant efforts of its editors at the Beethoven-Archiv in Bonn. Independently, Jonathan Del Mar has been making valuable critical editions of many works in recent years, and has earned just recognition for his assiduous labors.

Another task awaiting scholars is a new complete English translation of the Beethoven letters, replacing that of Emily Anderson, now that the annotated edition in German, edited by Sieghard Brandenburg, has been in print since 1998. Another is the continuing need for critical editions of the large number of sketchbooks that are still known only from their descriptions by Nottebohm and others, and the updated accounts in the reference book, *The Beethoven Sketchbooks*, by Douglas Johnson, Alan Tyson, and Robert Winter. Literally thousands of pages of sketches for major works remain to be made available in reliable transcription and facsimile.

Hand in hand with the study of the sketchbooks and sketch-leaves is the need for basic study of the many autograph manuscripts of Beethoven's works that contain late-stage changes in musical material as Beethoven strove to complete a given work. As a small sample of this immense territory, consider the innumerable changes of material that we see in the autograph manuscripts of the Fifth and Ninth symphonies, both of which have been available in facsimile editions for many years but are still awaiting closely detailed study of their late-stage changes. Related projects would bring us closer understanding of Beethoven's notational habits as he worked within his autographs; for example, his notation of dynamics and other expressive markings, on which new observations have recently been made by Nicholas Kitchen. A systematic expansion of our knowledge of this dimension is needed to help bridge the gap between scholarship and performance.

For the Conversation Books, as noted earlier, the primary source material in the original German is fully available, but its translation into English, now being undertaken by Theodore Albrecht, has just begun to appear in print. They offer unparalleled insight into the world of Beethoven's last period – his visitors, interlocutors, his daily life – and furnish a rich context for the late works, from 1818 to the end in 1827.

For now I leave it there, with the hope that students, scholars, and performers alike will continue to develop this supposedly well-worn field, knowing that they will find, as they do so, that new perspectives will emerge that will strengthen and transform understanding of the life and works of one of the enduring masters of Western music.

Bibliography

I. Primary Sources for Beethoven Biographies

Thematic Catalogues

Dorfmüller, Kurt, Norbert Gertsch, and Julia Ronge, (eds) *Ludwig van Beethoven, Thematisch-bibliographisches Werkverzeichnis*, 2 vols., Munich: G. Henle Verlag, 2014.

This massive reference work is the most recent thematic catalogue and supersedes all earlier similar catalogues, including that of Kinsky and Halm.

Kinsky, Georg, and Hans Halm, *Das Werk Beethovens: Thematisch-Bibliographisches Verzeichnis seiner sämtlichen vollendeten Kompositionen*, completed and edited by Hans Halm, Munich: G. Henle Verlag, 1955.

Letters

Ludwig van Beethoven, *Briefwechsel: Gesamtausgabe*, edited by Sieghard Brandenburg, 7 vols., Munich, G. Henle Verlag, 1996–98.

This collection of Beethoven's letters surpasses all earlier publications of the letters in German in its accuracy and completeness. Yet even now new letters may be discovered; an example is the important letter of 1795 to Heinrich von Struve, Bonn: Beethoven-Haus. NE 375, published by Julia Ronge (see "Ronge" in the third section of this Bibliography, "Related Books and Essays."

The Letters of Beethoven, 3 vols., translated and edited by Emily Anderson, London: Macmillan, 1961.

This is the largest collection of Beethoven's letters in English translation. A heroic achievement for its time, it nevertheless is now in need of revision in content and occasional matters of translation and dating.

Letters to Beethoven and Other Correspondence, translated and edited by Theodore Albrecht, 3 vols., Lincoln: University of Nebraska Press, 1996.

Conversation Books

Ludwig van Beethovens Konversationshefte, ed. Karl-Heinz Köhler, Grita Herre, and Dagmar Beck, 11 vols., Leipzig: VEB Deutscher Verlag fur Musik, 1972–2001.

The first complete edition of the Conversation Books.

Beethoven's Conversation Books, edited and translated by Theodore Albrecht, Woodbridge: The Boydell Press, in progress.

This projected complete translation into English is under way, and Volumes 1–3 have been published to date.

Memoirs

Breuning, Gerhard von, *Aus dem Schwarzspanierhause*, Vienna: Verlag von L. Rosner, 1874, and subsequent editions in German.
——, *Memories of Beethoven: From the House of the Black-Robed Spaniards*, ed. Maynard Solomon, Cambridge: Cambridge University Press, 1992.
Nohl, Ludwig, *Die Beethoven-Feier und die Kunst der Gegenwart*, Vienna: Braumuller, 1871.

Contains the text of this diary based on a copy made by Anton Gräffer (see the following essay by Maynard Solomon in *Beethoven Studies 3* for details).

Solomon, Maynard, "Beethoven's Tagebuch of 1812–1818," in *Beethoven Studies 3*, ed. Alan Tyson, Cambridge: Cambridge University Press, 1982, 193–288.

The complete text in German and English translation.

Solomon, Maynard, "Beethoven's Tagebuch" in his *Beethoven Essays*, Cambridge, MA: Harvard University Press, 1988, 233–95.

English only; the commentary is in part a revision of the 1982 publication.

Solomon, Maynard, *Beethovens Tagebuch*, ed. Sieghard Brandenburg, Bonn: Beethoven-Haus, 1990.

German only, with facsimiles of the known sources. On this edition see Solomon, *Beethoven*, 2nd edn (1998), 491.

Sketchbooks

Douglas Johnson, Alan Tyson, and Robert Winter, *The Beethoven Sketchbooks: History, Reconstruction., Inventory*, Berkeley: University of California Press, 1985.

An authoritative reference work that provided for the first time a complete inventory of the known Beethoven sketchbooks, their contents, techniques for reconstructing incomplete sketchbooks, and much more; an indispensable tool for later Beethoven sketch studies and thus for the close study of his creative work throughout his lifetime.

Impressions by Contemporaries

Kopitz, Klaus Martin and Rainer Cadenbach (eds), *Beethoven aus der Sicht seiner Zeitgenossen in Tagebüchern, Briefen, Gedichten und Erinnerungen*, 2 vols., Munich: G. Henle Verlag, 2009.

A comprehensive collection of personal commentaries on Beethoven as a man and artist, by a large number of his contemporaries.

II. Beethoven Biographies

Bekker, Paul, *Beethoven*, Berlin: Schuster & Löffler, 1912.

Caeyers, Jan, *Beethoven: een biografie*, Amsterdam: De Bezige Bij, 2009.

——, *Beethoven: Der einsame Revolutionär*, translated by Andreas Ecke, Munich: C. H. Beck, 2012.

Clubbe, John, *Beethoven: The Relentless Revolutionary*, New York: W. W. Norton, 2019.

Cooper, Barry, *Beethoven*, New York: Oxford University Press, 2000.

Cooper, Martin, *Beethoven: The Last Decade, 1817–1827*, Oxford: Oxford University Press, 1970: rev. edn, 1985.

Ernest, Gustav. *Beethoven: Persönlichkeit, Leben und Schaffen*, Berlin: G. Bondi, 1920.

Frimmel, Theodor, *Ludwig van Beethoven*, Berlin: "Harmonie," Verlagsgesellschaft für Literatur und Kunst, 1901.

Herriot, Edouard, *Vie de Beethoven*, Paris: Gallimard, 1929; translated by Adelheid I. Mitchell and William J. Mitchell as *The Life of Beethoven*, New York: Macmillan, 1935.

D'Indy, Vincent, *Beethoven: Biographie critique*, Paris: H. Laurens, 1911.

Kerman, Joseph and Alan Tyson, *The New Grove Beethoven*, New York: W. W. Norton, 1983.

Kinderman, William, *Beethoven*, Berkeley: University of California Press, 1995.

——, *Beethoven*, 2nd edn, Oxford: Oxford University Press, 2009.

Korte, Werner, *L. van. Beethoven*, Berlin: Max Hesses Verlag, 1936.

Kropfinger, Klaus, *Beethoven*, Kassel: Bärenreiter, 2001.

Küster, Konrad, *Beethoven*, Stuttgart: Deutsche Verlags-Anstalt, 1994.

Lenz, Wilhelm von, *Beethoven et ses trois styles*, St. Petersburg: Bernard, 1852–3.

——, *Beethoven: Eine Kunst-Studie*, 5 vols., Hamburg: Hoffmann & Co., 1860.

Lockwood, Lewis, *Beethoven: The Music and the Life*, New York: W. W. Norton, 2003.

Marek, George, *Beethoven: Biography of a Genius*, New York: Thomas Y. Crowell, 1969.

Marx, Adolf Bernhard, *Ludwig van Beethoven: Leben und Schaffen*, Berlin: Otto Janke, 1859; reprint, Hildesheim and New York: Georg Olms, 1979.

Morris, Edmund, *Beethoven: The Universal Composer*, New York: Harper Collins, 2005.

Nohl, Ludwig, *Beethovens Leben*, 3 vols., Vienna: Vienna,: Markgraf & Müller, 1864 and Leipzig: Günther, 1867–77. Published in English as *Life of Beethoven*, translated by John J. Labor, Chicago: A. C. McClurg, 1892.

Prod'homme, Jacques, *Les symphonies de Beethoven (1800 – 1827)*, Paris: C. Delagrave, 1906.

Riezler, Walter, *Beethoven*, translated by G. D. H. Pidock, London: M. C. Forester, 1938. [First published in Berlin and Zurich: Atlantis Verlag, 1936.]

Rolland, Romain, *Vie de Beethoven*, Paris: Hachette, 1907.

——, *Beethoven: Les grands époques créatices*, 6 vols., Paris: Saliber, 1928–45.

Schindler, Anton F., *Biographie von Ludwig van Beethoven*, Münster: Aschendorff, 1840. [2nd edn, 1845. 3rd edn, 1860. Published in English as *Beethoven as I Knew Him*, trans. Constance S. Jolly, ed. Donald W. MacArdle. Chapel Hill: University of North Carolina Press, 1966.]

Schiedermair, Ludwig, *Der junge Beethoven*, Leipzig: Quelle & Meyer, 1925.

Schlosser, Johann Aloys, *Ludwig van Beethoven. Eine Biographie desselben, verbunden mit Urtheilen über seine werke*, Prague: Buchler, Stephani & Schlosser, 1827; rev. 2nd printing, 1828. Trans. into English by Reinhard G. Pauly as *Beethoven: The First Biography*, ed. Barry Cooper, Portland: Amadeus Press, 1996.

Schmitz, Arnold, *Beethoven*, Bonn: Verlag der Buchgemeinde, 1927.

——, *Das romantische Beethovenbild: Darstellung und Kritik*, Berlin and Bonn: Dümmler, 1927; reprinted 1978.

Scott, Marion, *Beethoven*, London: J. M. Dent and Sons Ltd., 1934.

Sullivan, J. W. N., *Beethoven: His Spiritual Development*, London and New York: Knopf, 1927.

Solomon, Maynard, *Beethoven*, New York: Schirmer Books, 1977. 2nd edn, 1998.

——, *Late Beethoven: Music, Thought, Imagination*, Berkeley: University of California Press, 2003.

Swafford, Jan, *Beethoven: Anguish and Triumph*, New York: Houghton Mifflin Harcourt, 2014.

Thayer, Alexander Wheelock, *Ludwig van Beethovens Leben*, ed. Hermann Deiters, 3 vol. Berlin: Weber, 1866–79. [2nd edn Hugo Riemann; Berlin: Breitkopf & Härtel, 1907–15. English edn H. E. Krehbiel from Thayer's notes, 3 vols., New York: Beethoven Association, 1921. Rev. edn Elliot Forbes as *Thayer's Life of Beethoven*; Princeton: Princeton University Press, 1964.]

Thomas-San-Galli, Wolfgang Alexander, *Ludwig van Beethoven*, Munich: R. Piper, 1913.

Tovey, Donald Francis, *Beethoven*, London: Oxford University Press, 1944.

Wagner, Richard, *Beethoven*, Leipzig: Fritsch, 1870. [Translated by Roger Allen as *Richard Wagner's Beethoven (1870)*, Woodbridge: The Boydell Press, 2014.]

Wegeler, Franz Gerhard and Ferdinand Ries, *Biographische Notizen über Ludwig van Beethoven*, Coblenz: Bädeher, 1838 and 1845; reprinted, Hildesheim: Georg Olms, 2000. [Translated into French by Gottfried Engelbert Anders as "Détails biographiques sur Beethoven d'après Wegeler et Ries," Paris: *Revue et Gazette Musicale*, 1839.]

Wyn Jones, David, *The Life of Beethoven*, Cambridge: Cambridge University Press, 1998.

III. Related Books and Essays

Adorno, Theodor W., *Beethoven: The Philosophy of Music*, ed. Rolf Tiedemann, Stanford: Stanford University Press, 1998.

Agmon, Eytan, "Beethoven's Op. 81a and the Psychology of Loss," *Music Theory Online* 2/4 May 1996.

Albrecht, Theodore, "Thayer contra Marx: A Warning from 1860; An Edited Reprint of Thayer's Review of Marx's Beethoven Biography," *Beethoven Journal* 14, no. 1 (Summer 1999), 2–8; 14, no. 2 (Winter 1999), 56–64.

——, "Anton Schindler as Destroyer and Forger of Beethoven's Conversation Books," in *Music's Intellectual History*, 169–181, ed. Zdravko Blažeković, New York: Répertoire International de la Littérature Musicale, 2009.

Allen, Roger, *Richard Wagner's Beethoven (1870)*, Woodbridge: The Boydell Press, 2014.

Angermüller, Rudolph et al., *Beethoven-Studien: Festgabe der Oesterreichischen Akademie der Wissenschaften zum 200. Geburtstag von Ludwig van Beethoven*, Vienna: Hermann Boehlaus Nachfolger, 1970.

Barth, George, *The Pianist as Orator: Beethoven and the Transformation of Keyboard Style*, Ithaca: Cornell University Press, 1992.

Beck, Dagmar and Grita Herre, "Einige Zweifel an der Überlieferung der Konversationshefte," in *Bericht über den Internationalen Beethoven-Kongress Berlin 1977*. 257–69, Leipzig: Deutscher Verlag fur Musik, 1978.

——, "Anton Schindlers fingierte Eintragungen in den Konversationsheften," in *Zu Beethoven: Aufsätze und Annotationen*. Vol. 1, 11–89, ed. Harry Goldschmidt, Berlin: Verlag Neue Musik, 1979.

Bekker, Paul, Review of Heinrich Schenker's "Musiker Faksimiles" / Moonlight Sonata," *Musikblätter des Anbruch*, Vienna: Universal-Edition, February and April 1922. The German text and an English translation by Ian Bent and

William Drabkin can be found at Schenkerdocumentson-line.org

Beethoven-Symposium Wien 1970, Vienna: Hermann Böhlaus Nachfolger, 1971.

Bellofatto, Luigi, *Alexander Wheelock Thayer: The Greatest Biographer of Ludwig van Beethoven*, Lewiston, NY: Edwin Mellen Press, 2010.

Berlioz, Hector, *A Critical Study of Beethoven's Nine Symphonies with a Few words on His Trios and Sonatas, a Criticism of Fidelio, and an Introductory Essay on Music*, translated into English by Edwin Evans, introduction by D. Kern Holoman, Urbana: University of Illinois Press, 2000.

Bormann, Patrick, *Das Bonner Beethoven-Haus 1933–1945*, Bonn: Beethoven-Haus, 2016.

Boyle, Nicholas, *Goethe: The Poet and the Age*, 2 vols., Oxford: Clarendon Press, 1991, 2002.

Brenneis, Clemens, "Das Fischhof Manuskript: Zur Frühgeschichte der Beethoven-Biographik," in *Zu Beethoven: Aufsätze und Annotationen*, 90–116, ed. H. Goldschmidt, Berlin: Verlag Neue Musik, 1979.

Brenneis, Clemens (ed.), *Ludwig van Beethoven: Ein Skizzenbuch aus dem Jahre 1809*, 2 vols., Bonn: Beethoven-Haus, 1993.

Brenner, Daniel, *Anton Schindler und sein Einfluss auf die Beethoven-Biographik*, Bonn: Verlag Beethoven-Haus, 2013.

Burnham, Scott, *Beethoven Hero*, Princeton: Princeton University Press, 1995.

——, "The four ages of Beethoven: critical reception and the canonic composer" in Glenn Stanley (ed.), *The Cambridge Companion to Beethoven*, Cambridge: Cambridge University Press, 2000, 272–91.

Clive, Peter, *Beethoven and His World: A Biographical Dictionary*, Oxford: Oxford University Press, 2001.

Comini, Alessandra, *The Changing Image of Beethoven: A Study in Mythmaking*, New York: Rizzoli, 1987.

Cook, Grant W. III., "Alexander Wheelock Thayer: A New Biographical Sketch," *The Beethoven Journal* 17, no. 1 (Summer 2002), 2–11.

——, "Expatriates in Trieste: Letter from Sir Richard Francis and Isabel Burton to Alexander Wheelock Thayer." *The Beethoven Journal* 21, no. 2 (Winter 2006), 4–9.

——, "Dwight's'Diarist' and '"John," a Portland boy.' The 1858 Trans-Atlantic voyage of Alexander Wheelock Thayer and John Knowles Paine," *The Beethoven Journal* 23, no. 1 (Summer 2008) 4–14.

——, "The Cramer Narrative Revisited. A New Letter from Alexander Wheelock Thayer to Robert Edward Lonsdale (1868)," *The Beethoven Journal* 23, no. 2 (Winter 2008) 74–8.

——, "The Final American Residency of Beethoven's Biographer Alexander Wheelock Thayer," *The Beethoven Journal* 27, no. 2 (Winter 2012), 64–73.

——, "The Final American Residency of Beethoven's Biographer Alexander Wheelock Thayer. Part II: July 1857 through July 1858," *The Beethoven Journal* 28 no. 1 (Summer 2013), 26–33.

——, "'I was now in the birthplace of Beethoven': The First European Research Expedition of Alexander Wheelock Thayer, 1849–1851," *The Beethoven Journal* 31, no. 2 (Winter 2016), 71–82.

Cooper, Barry, *Beethoven and the Creative Process*, Oxford: Clarendon Press, 1990.

——, (ed.) *The Beethoven Compendium: A Guide to Beethoven's Life and Music*, London: Thames and Hudson, 1991.

——, *Beethoven's Folksong Settings: Chronology, Sources, Style*, Oxford: Clarendon Press, 1994.

——, Review of *The Life of Beethoven*, by David Wyn Jones. *Music & Letters* 80, no. 4 (1999), 629–31.

Dahlhaus, Carl, *Nineteenth-Century Music*, translated by J. Bradford Robinson, Berkley CA: University of California Press, 1989.

——, *Beethoven: Approaches to His Music*, Oxford: Clarendon Press, 1991.

Dennis, David, *Beethoven in German Politics, 1870–1989*, New Haven: Yale University Press, 1996.

——, *Inhumanities: Nazi Interpretations of Western Culture*, Cambridge: Cambridge University Press, 2012.

Drabkin, William, Review of *The Life of Beethoven*, by David Wyn Jones, *The Musical Times* 140, no. 1867 (Summer 1999), 69–70.

——, Review of *Beethoven*, by Barry Cooper, *19th-Century Music* 26, no. 1 (Summer 2002), 94–110.

Frimmel, Theodor, *Beethoven und Goethe: Eine Studie*, Vienna: Druck und Verlag von Carl Gerold's Sohn, 1883.

——, *Neue Beethoveniana*, Vienna: C. Gerold's Sohn, 1888.

——, *Beethoven-Handbuch*, 2 vols., Leipzig: Breitkopf & Härtel, 1926; Reprinted in one volume by Georg Olms Verlag, Hildesheim: Verlag AG, 2003.

Gooch, G. P., *History and Historians in the Nineteenth Century*, 3rd edn, London: Longmans, Green, and Co., 1920.

Graves, Charles L., *The Life & Letters of Sir George Grove*, London: Macmillan, 1903.

Grove, George, *A Dictionary of Music and Musicians (A.D. 1450–1889)*, 4 vols., London and New York: MacMillan, 1879–90.

——, *Beethoven, Schubert, Mendelssohn*, Introduction by Eric Blom, London: Macmillan, 1951.

Hallé, Charles, *The Autobiography of Charles Hallé, with Correspondence and Diaries*, ed. Michael Kennedy. New York: Barnes & Noble, 1973.

Hanheide, Stefan, "Die Beethoven-Interpretation von Romain Rolland und ihre methodischen Grundlagen," *Archiv für Musikwissenchaft* 61, no. 4 (2004), 255–74.

Holmes, Richard, *This Long Pursuit: Reflections of a Romantic Biographer*, London: William Collins, 2016.

Kerman, Joseph, "Tovey's Beethoven," in *Beethoven Studies 2*, ed. Alan Tyson. Oxford: Oxford University Press, 1977.

——, "Sketch Studies," in *Musicology in the 1980s: Methods, Goals, Opportunities*, ed. D. Kern Holoman and Claude V. Palisca, New York: Da Capo Press, 1982, 53–66

Kinderman, William (ed.), *Artaria 195: Beethoven's Sketchbook for the "Missa Solemnis" and the Piano Sonata in E Major, Opus 109*, 3 vols., Urbana: University of Illinois Press, 2003.

Knittel, K. M., "Imitation, Individuality, and Illness: Beethoven's Three Styles," *Beethoven Forum* 4, no. 1 (1995), 17–36.

Korsyn, Kevin, "J. W. N. Sullivan and the *Heiliger Dankgesang*: Questions of Meaning in Late Beethoven," *Beethoven Forum* 2 (1993), 133–76.

Krauss, B. A., *Die Beethoven-Rezeption in Frankreich: Von ihren Anfängen bis zum Untergang des Second Empire*, Bonn: Beethoven-Haus, 2001.

——, "L'homme et l'Œuvre? Der Französische Beethoven," *Bonner Beethoven-Studien* 4 (2005), 71–89.

Kroll, Mark, *Ignaz Moscheles and the Changing World of Musical Europe*,Woodbridge: Boydell Press, 2014.

Kropfinger, Klaus, *Wagner and Beethoven: Richard Wagner's Reception of Beethoven*, Cambridge: Cambridge University Press, 1991.

Lockspeiser, Edward, "Vincent d'Indy and Beethoven," *The Listener* 52 (October 7, 1954), 593.

Lockwood, Lewis, "Nottebohm Revisited," *Current Thought in Musicology*, ed John W. Grubbs. Austin: University of Texas Press, 1976, 139–92.

——, *Beethoven: Studies in the Creative Process*, Cambridge, MA: Harvard University Press, 1992.

——, "Beethoven, Florestan, and the Varieties of Heroism," in *Beethoven and His World*, ed. Scott Burnham and

Michael P. Steinberg, Princeton: Princeton University Press, 2000, 27–47.

——, *Beethoven's Symphonies: An Artistic Vision*, New York: W. W. Norton, 2015.

Lockwood, Lewis, and Alan Gosman (eds), *Beethoven's "Eroica" Sketchbook: A Critical Edition*, 2 vols., Urbana: University of Illinois Press, 2013.

Loos, Helmut, "Arnold Schmitz as Beethoven Scholar: A Reassessment," *Journal of Musicological Research* 32, nos. 2–3 (April 2013), 150–62.

Lühning, Helga, "Das Schindler und das Beethoven-Bild," *Bonner Beethoven-Studien* 2 (2001), 183–99.

Marshall, Robert L, *Mozart Speaks: Views on Music, Musicians, and the World*, New York: Schirmer Books, 1991.

Millington, Barry, (ed.), *The Wagner Compendium*, London: Thames and Hudson, 1992.

Mitchell, Greg, "A Fuller Love for Beethoven," *Pressing Issues*. Blog post. April 17, 2014. http://gregmitchellwriter.blog-spot.com/2014/04/a-fuller-love-for-beethoven.html.

Niemetschek, Franz, *Life of Mozart (Lebens des K. K. Kapellmeisters Wolfgang Gottlieb Mozart, 1798)*, translated by Helen Mautner, London: Leonard Hyman, 1956.

Nohl, Ludwig, *Beethoven's Brevier*, Leipzig: Günther, 1870.

——, *Beethoven, Liszt, Wagner*, Vienna: Wilhelm Braumüller, 1874.

Nottebohm, Gustav, *Thematisches Verzeichnis der im Druck erschienenen Werke von Ludwig van Beethoven*, Leipzig: Breitkopf & Härtel, 1868.

Pais, Abraham, *"Subtle is the Lord...": The Science and the Life of Albert Einstein*, Oxford: Oxford University Press, 1982.

Potter, Pamela M, *Most German of the Arts: Musicology and Society from the Weimar Republic to the End of Hitler's Reich*, New Haven and London: Yale University Press, 1998.

Ronge, Julia, *Beethovens Lehrzeit: Kompositionsstudien bei Joseph Haydn, Johann Georg Albrechtsberger und Antonio Salieri*, Bonn: Beethoven-Haus, 2011.

——, "wann wird auch der Zeitpunkt kommen wo es nur Menschen geben wird: Ein unbekannter Brief Beethovens an Heinrich von Struve," *Jahresgabe des Beethoven-Hauses Bonn* Heft 34 (2018).

Rosen, Charles, *The Classical Style: Haydn, Mozart, Beethoven*, expanded edn, New York: W. W. Norton, 1997.

Sadie, Stanley and Nigel Fortune, *The New Grove Dictionary of Music and Musicians*, 20 vols., London: Macmillan, 1980.

Saloman, Ora Frishberg, *Beethoven's Symphonies and J. S. Dwight*, Boston: Northeastern University Press, 1995.

Scurr, Ruth, "The Part of the Whole: A Spectrum of Approaches to Autobiography," *The Times Literary Supplement*, October 26, 2018.

Schindler, Anton, *Beethoven in Paris*, Münster: Aschendorff, 1842.

Schmidt, Christian Martin, *Johannes Brahms und seine Zeit*, Laaber: Laaber-Verlag, 1983.

Schmitz, Arnold, *Beethovens "Zwei Prinzipe": ihre Bedeutung für Themen- und Satzbau*, Berlin: Dümmlers Verlagbuchhandlung, 1923.

Schoenbaum, Samuel, *Shakespeare's Lives*, New edn Oxford: Oxford University Press, 1991.

Schrade, Leo, *Beethoven in France*, New Haven: Yale University Press, 1942.

Seigel, Jerrold, *Modernity and Bourgeois Life*, Cambridge: Cambridge University Press, 2012.

Shapiro, James, *Contested Will: Who Wrote Shakespeare*, New York: Simon and Schuster, 2010.

Solomon, Maynard, "Sonneck and Krehbiel: A Beethoven Correspondence," in *Beethoven Essays: Studies in Honor of Elliot Forbes*, edited by Lewis Lockwood and Phyllis

Benjamin, Cambridge: Harvard University Department of Music, 1984, 66–77.

——, *Beethoven Essays*, Cambridge, MA: Harvard University Press, 1988.

Stadlen, Peter, "Schindler's Beethoven Forgeries," *The Musical Times* 118, no. 1613 (July 1977), 256–52.

Stanley, Glenn, "Some thoughts on biography and a chronology of Beethoven's life and music," in *The Cambridge Companion to Beethoven*, ed. Glenn Stanley, Cambridge: Cambridge University Press, 2000, 1–13.

Steblin, Rita, "Reminiscences of Beethoven in Anton Gräffer's unpublished memoirs: a legacy of the Viennese biography project of 1827," *Bonner Beethoven-Studien* 4 (2005), 149–89.

Stern, Fritz, *Five Germanys I Have Known*, New York: Farrar, Straus, and Giroux, 2006.

Thayer, Alexander Wheelock, "Schindler's Life of Beethoven," *The Musical World* 38, no. 1 (January 7, 1860), 12–13.

——, Review of *Ludwig van Beethoven: Leben und Schaffen*, by A. B. Marx, *Atlantic Monthly* 5, no. 30 (April 1860), 497–505.

——, *Ein Kritischer Beitrag zur Beethoven-Literatur*, Berlin: W. Weber, 1877.

Tyson, Alan, *The Authentic English Editions of Beethoven*, London: Faber & Faber, 1963.

——, "Ferdinand Ries (1784–1838), The History of His Contribution to Beethoven Biography," *19th-Century Music* 7, no. 3 (April 3, 1984), 209–21.

Ullrich, Hermann, "Karl Holz, Beethovens letzter Freund," *Studien zur Musikwissenschaft* 31 (January 1, 1980), 67–189.

Wagner, Richard, *Sämtliche Briefe Vol. I: 1830–42*, ed. Gertrud Strobel and Werner Wolf, Leipzig: Deutscher Verlag für Musik, 1967.

——, "A Pilgrimage to Beethoven," *Revue et gazette musicale*, November–December 1840, English translation by William Ashton Ellis, *Richard Wagner's Prose Works*, London: Kegan Paul, Trench, Trübner & Co. Ltd., 1898, vol. 7, 21–45.

——, *Mein Leben*, Translated by Andrew Gray as *My Life*, Cambridge: Cambridge University Press, 1983.

Young, Percy, *George Grove 1820–1900: A Biography*, London: Macmillan, 1980.

Young-Bruehl, Elisabeth, "The Writing of Biography," *Partisan Review* 50, no. 3 (1983), 413. Reprinted in *Mind and the Body Politic*, New York: Routledge, 1989, 125–37.

——, *Anna Freud: A Biography*, New York: Summit Books, 1988.

Index

Agmon, Eytan 159 n.38
Albrecht, Theodore 12 n.16,
    16 n.3, 19 n.6, n.7, 26, 38
    n.45, 46, 182
Albrechtsberger, Johann
    Georg 20 n.10, 47
Alcoholism 107, 147, 154
Allen, Roger 53 n.76
Ambros, August Wilhelm
    von 38
Anders, Gottfried
    Engelbert 51, 53-4, 87
Anderson, Emily 5 n.6, 11
    n.13, 19 n.8,107, 136, 156
    n.27, 157 n.30, 159 n.37,
    162 n.43, 174 nn.7,8, 181
Anschütz, Heinrich 1
Arnim, Bettina von 107
Artaria 8, 132 n.25

Bach, Johann Baptist 19
Bach, Johann Sebastian 2,
    38, 66, 79, 92, 148, 177
    Well-Tempered
        Clavier 148
Bach-Gesellschaft
    Edition 38
Badura-Skoda, Eva 22 n.12,
    116
Baez, Joan 119
Balzac, Honoré de 86
Barbadette, Henry 90
Barth, George 22 n.12

Bartók, Béla 66
Beck, Dagmar 26, 27 n.24-
    6, 116
Beethoven Family
    Beethoven, Ludwig van
        (grandfather) 147, 169
    Beethoven, Johann van
        (father) 107, 120, 147,
        151
    Beethoven, Maria
        Magdalena
        (mother) 147, 151, 154,
    Beethoven, Johann
        (brother) 9, 19, 40, 74
    Beethoven, Caspar Carl
        van (brother) 6, 40, 74,
        164
    Beethoven, Johanna (sister-
        in-law) 6, 164
    Beethoven, Karl
        (nephew) 6, 8, 12, 19,
        25, 71, 118, 120, 162, 163,
        164f
    Beethoven, Ludwig van
    Catalogues
        Breitkopf & Härtel 34f
        Dorfmüller-Gertsch-
            Ronge 36, 37 n.44
        Hess 37 n.43
        Johnson-Tyson-
            Winter 127
        Kinsky-Halm 36, 37
            n.44

Lenz   42

Nottebohm   35 n.39,
   36, 37 n.44, 42

Thayer   34, 35, 37, 42,
   49

Wagner-Anders
   [proposed]   55

Conversation Books   3,
   4, 5, 7, 13, 16 n.3, 17, 23,
   25f, 27, 28, 29, 30, 32, 41,
   112, 116, 118, 140, 172, 173,
   179, 181

Health

   General   7 n.9, 151, 154

   Deafness   1, 10, 25 n.20,
      46, 65, 74, 79, 95, 96,
      97, 120, 123, 127, 136,
      137, 154

   Death   1, 10, 19, 20, 22,
      27, 29 n.20, 33, 65, 115,
      122, 162, 165

   Final year   10, 12, 19,
      20, 21, 25, 162f, 164

Heiligenstadt

   Testament   45, 79, 81,
      96, 98, 114, 120, 122, 132

Image   1, 15, 65, 66, 67 n.2,
   82, 103, 105f

"Immortal Beloved"
   question   45, 79, 81, 89,
   115, 121, 122, 135, 140

Old age   13, 18, 19f, 72, 118,
   122, 162-5, 168

Patrons

   Archduke Rudolph   111,
      138, 139, 147, 154, 156,
      157, 158 n.31, 159, 161,
      173, 180

Count August von
   Hatzfeld   148

Count Andreas
   Razumovsky   156

Count Ferdinand
   Waldstein   148, 149

Elector Maximilian
   Franz   147, 151, 153
   n.21

Prince Nikolaus
   Galitzin   163

Prince Ferdinand
   Kinsky   156, 157

Prince Karl
   Lichnowsky   156

Prince Franz Joseph
   Lobkowitz   156f

Personality   2f, 4f, 10, 12f,
   21, 38, 46, 48, 65, 70f, 74f,
   97, 98, 120f, 122f, 128,
   129, 133, 134, 135f, 151,
   154, 157, 159f, 161f, 163,
   165, 169, 171ff, 176

Tagebuch   45, 118, 122f,
   136

Youth   81, 97, 108, 116, 128,
   140, 146-154, 166

Beethoven, biography, larger
   trends   129

Beethoven Verein   73

Beethoven, Ludwig van,
   works

   "An die ferne Geliebte" Op.
      98   108, 125

   Bagatelles Op. 126   47

   Cello Sonata Op. 69   99

   Choral Fantasy Op.
      80   155

Christus am Ölberge Op.
    85   114 n.26
Concertos
    Piano and orchestra Op.
        19   152
    Piano and orchestra Op.
        58   99, 139, 155, 160
        n.39
    Piano and orchestra Op.
        73   161
    Piano and orchestra
        WoO 4   152
    Violin and Orchestra
        Op. 61   99, 139
Fantasie for piano, Op.
    77   161
Fidelio   91, 111, 133, 179
Folksongs   90, 134
Für Elise WoO 59   45
Leonore Overtures   21 n.
    11, 39
Mass in C major Op.
    86   158
Missa Solemnis Op.
    123   23, 30, 111, 158, 160
    n.39, 173
Piano Sonatas   42, 89, 134
    Piano Sonatas WoO
        47   134, 152
    Piano Sonatas Op.
        2   154
    Piano Sonata Op. 13   28
    Piano Sonata Op. 27 No.
        2   80
    Piano Sonata Op. 31 No.
        3   114 n.26
    Piano Sonata Op.
        53   95

Piano Sonata Op.
    78   161
Piano Sonata Op.
    79   161
Piano Sonata Op. 81a
    "Lebewohl"   159, 161
Piano Sonata Op.
    101   80
Piano Sonata Op.
    106   122, 133, 160
    n.39
Piano Sonata Op.
    111   133, 160 n.39
Quartets   7, 125f
    Quartets, Op. 18   83
    Quartets, Op. 59   113,
        128, 139
    Quartet, Op. 74   83, 99,
        155 n. 23, 161
    Quartet, Op. 95   83
    Quartet, Op. 130   163f
        Große Fuge   158, 160
        n.39, 163f
    Quartet, Op. 131   163,
        164
    Quartet Op. 132   133
    Quartet, Op. 135   6,
        128, 163, 164
Quintets
    Quintet for Piano and
        Strings Op. 16   133
    Quintet for Strings Op.
        29   175
    Quintet for Strings
        WoO 62   164
Symphonies   33 n. 34, 66,
    86, 89
    Symphony No. 2   96

Symphony No. 3   83,
  84, 98f, 111, 114, 133,
  158, 173
Symphony No. 4   83,
  98, 99, 139
Symphony No. 5   47,
  80, 83, 84, 98f, 104,
  138, 155, 181
Symphony No. 6   83,
  98f, 155, 160
Symphony No. 7   83,
  98f, 122
Symphony No. 8   28,
  83, 98f, 1221
Symphony No. 9   7, 11,
  19, 30, 52, 56, 84, 99,
  103, 111, 173, 181
Trios
  Piano Trios Op. 1   154
  "Archduke" Piano Trio,
    Op. 97   99
  String Trio, Op. 3   90
  String Trio, Op. 70
    No. 2   99
Variations for Piano in C
  minor WoO 80   139
Violin Sonata Op. 96   99
"Diabelli" Variations for
  Piano Op. 120   30, 180
Sketchbooks
  MS Artaria 195   132
    n.25
  "Eroica
    Sketchbook"   132
    n.25
  "Fischhof"
    Miscellany   7 n. 9,

8 n.11, 9 n.12, 116, 152
  n. 20
"Grasnick 5"   132 n.25
Kafka Miscellany   126
"Kessler
  Sketchbook"   17
"Landsberg 5"   161 n.41
"Wielhorsky
  Sketchbook"   114
"Wittgenstein
  Sketchbook"   29 n.30
Bekker, Paul   69, 77-80, 81,
  93, 100, 107
Bellofatto, Luigi   31 n.33, 35
  n.39, 40 n.49, 46 n.62, 70
  n.6, 73 n.13, 74 n.16, 75
  n.18
Benedict, Sir Julius   3f
Bent, Ian   80 n.28, 130 n.23
Bent, Margaret   111 n.19
Benjamin, Phyllis   71n7
Berger, Ludwig   50
Berger, Wilhelm   81
Berlioz, Hector   23, 54, 86, 89
Berlin   29, 30, 34, 35, 50, 73,
  77, 112, 114-6, 180,
Bhagavad-Gita   123
Biba, Otto   112, 116
Bischoff, Ludwig   56
Bismarck, Otto von   65
Blažeković, Zdravko   16 n.3
Blom, Eric   92 n. 56
Bogner, Elisabeth von   29
  n.9
Bonaparte, Napoleon   89,
  108, 156, 158, 173, 175, 180
Bonaparte, Jerome   156

Bonn 9, 10, 11, 12, 34, 38, 53, 70, 73, 81, 82, 106, 107, 127, 136, 147, 148, 149, 150, 151, 152, 153, 154
Bonn, Beethoven commemoration 68
Bonn, Beethoven Conference 1970 112f, 113 n.22, 114 n.26, 116
Bonn, Beethoven-Haus 5, 36, 104
Bonn, monument to Beethoven 9, 17, 24
Beethoven-Verein 73
Bonn, musical life 151
Bormann, Patrick 104 n.3, 106 n.8, 107
Boyle, Nicholas 170
Brahms, Johannes 23f, 35 n.42, 50, 73, 79, 81
Brandenburg, Sieghard 112, 113, 122 n.10, 126, 137, 156 n.28, 160 n.40, 181,
Breitkopf & Härtel 34, 36, 37 n.44, 38, 54, 68 n.3, 77 n.22, 155, 158, 160, 161
Brendel, Franz 23
Brenneis, Clemens 7 n.9, 8, 9 n.12, 116, 161 n.41
Brenner, Daniel 15 n.1, 16 n.3, 18 n.4, 19 n.7, 22 n.12, 23 n.14, 26 n.21, 29 n.31, 43 n.55, 53 n.79-80, 54 n.82, 79 n.26
Brentano, Antonie 115, 121, 135
Breuning, Eleonore von 10

Breuning, Gerhard von 12-3, 122
Breuning, Stephan von 8, 25
Brook Farm 33
Brunswick, Therese 79
Bücken, Ernst 107
Burnham, Scott 1 n.2, 44, 99 n.67
Burrow, Colin 170

Cadenbach, Rainer 2 n.3, 3 n.4, 4 n.5
Cannadine, David 92 n. 54
Carlyle, Thomas 33
Carr, Bruce 116 n.29
Chopin, Frédéric 23, 54
Churgin, Bathia 124 n.13
Clement, Franz 180
Clementi, Muzio 180
Clive, Peter 20 n.9, 91 n.51, 149 n.10, 13
Comini, Alessandra 1 n.1, 106 n.6
Coldicott, Anne-Louise 77 n.23, 134
Collier, John Payne 30
Cook III, Grant William A 31 n.33, 34 n.37, 39 n.48, 40 nn.49,51
Cooper, Barry 7 n.9, 77, 90 n.50, 134-6, 144, 155 n.23, 173 n.6
Cooper, Martin 118
Czerny, Carl 11

Dahlhaus, Carl 24 n.16, 79, 113 n.22, 146, 170
Debussy, Claude 66, 89

de Gaulle, Charles   85f
Dehn, Siegfried   50
Deiters, Hermann   17, 34
    n.38, 49, 55, 69, 70, 71, 72,
    81, 105
Del Mar, Jonathan   36, 181
Dennis, David   103 n.1, 105,
    106, 109 n.14
Deym, Josephine   121
D'Indy, Vincent   69, 85, 87-9
Dorfmüller, Kurt   36, 37n44
Dorn, Heinrich   40
Drabkin, William   77 n.23,
    80 n.28, 84 n.36, 134, 135
    n.32, 136
Dunsby, Jonathan   130 n.24
Duport, Jean Louis   18
Dürer, Albrecht   65
Dussek, Jan Ladislav   180
Dwight, John Sullivan   33,
    34, 40, 46 n.62-3, 73, 74

Edison, Thomas   67, 137
Eggebrecht, Hans
    Heinrich   67
Eibner, Franz   112
Eliot, Thomas Stearns   96
Ernest, Gustav   69, 80-1

Ferraguto, Mark   137, 139,
    145
"Fischhof" manuscript   116
Fishman, Nathan   114
Forbes, Elliot   69 n.4, 70, 71
    n.7, 72, 73, 117 n.1
Fortune, Nigel   87 n.43, 92 n.
Freud, Anna   23, 175 n.9
Freud, Sigmund   23, 119, 126

Fricke, W.   68
Frimmel, Theodor   64, 68
    n.3, 69, 75f, 77, 81, 137
Fuller, Margaret   33

Gardiner, William   90
Gassner, Ferdinand   7
Gerigk, Herbert   110
Gertsch, Norbert   36, 37
    n.44
Giannatasio, Fanny   45 n.59
Gibbs, Christopher   1 n.2
Gluck, Christoph Willibald
    von   42, 89
Goethe, Johann Wolfgang
    von   32, 65, 75, 80, 109,
    128, 170
Goldschmidt, Harry   7, 27
Gosman, Alan   132 n.25
Gräffer, Anton   8
Grigat, Friederike   22 n.13
Grillparzer, Franz   1-3, 165
    funeral oration   1
Grove, George   70, 90, 92-3,
    101, 123
Guicciardi, Giulietta   79

Habeneck, François   86
Haberl, Dieter   140, 150
Hallé, Charles   1
Halm, Hans   36, 37 n.44
Handel, Georg Frideric   2
Hanheide, Stefan   88 n.44
Haslinger, Tobias   4
Haydn, Franz Joseph   2, 8,
    20 n.10, 44, 47, 83, 92,
    95, 113 n.25, 118, 126 n.18,
    128, 137, 149

Heine, Heinrich   29, 53
Henle Verlag   36, 128, 180
Herre, Grita   26, 27, 116
Herriot, Edouard   89
Hess, Willy   36 n. 43
Hiller, Ferdinand   21, 22
Hirsch, Carl Friedrich   76
Hitler, Adolf   103, 104 n.3
Holoman, D. Kern   108 n.39
Holmes, Richard   170
Holz, Karl   5ff, 9, 10, 13, 19,
    20 n.9, 57, 163
Hotschevar, Jakob   8
Hugo, Victor   86
Hummel, Johann
    Nepomuk   21, 180
Huxley, Aldous   96

Ireland, William Henry   30

Jahn, C. F.   68
Jahn, Otto   35, 38, 75
Jeitteles, Alois   108
Joachim, Joseph   24, 73
Johnson, Douglas   29, 50
    n.70, 115, 116, 126f, 152
    n.20, 181
Jones, David Wyn   136f, 179
Judt, Tony   108

Kagan, Susan   157 n.31, 158
    n.33, 180
Kelly, Elaine   109
Kerman, Joseph   42, 94,
    123ff, 143
Kiesewetter, Raphael   38
Kinderman, William   132f,
    144, 155 n.23

King Lear   4, 145
Kinsky, Georg   36, 37 n. 44
Kirby, F.E.   117 n.1
Kirkendale, Warren   111
Kitchen, Nicholas   181
Klein, Rudolph   112 n.21
Knittel, Kristin   7 n.9, 43 n.54
Köhler, Karl-Heinz   26, 116
Kojima, Shin
    Augustinus   112
Kopitz, Klaus Martin   2 n.3,
    3 n.4, 4 n.5
Korsyn, Kevin   96 n.62, 97
Korte, Werner   107f
Kraft, Anton   180
Kraft, Nikolaus   180
Kramer, Richard   112, 113,
    116 n.29
Krauss, Beate Angelica   87
Krehbiel, Henry Edward   69
    n.4, 70, 71ff
Kroll, Mark   18 n.5, 91 n.52
Kropfinger, Klaus   52 n.74,
    54, 56, 123, 124, 128f
Kross, Siegfried   112
Kunze, Stefan   179
Kurth, Sabine   164 n.45v

Larkin, Edward   118f
Larsen, Jens Peter   112 n.20
Lenz, Wilhelm von   7, 16, 17,
    18, 21, 35, 41, 42f, 56, 163
Lincoln, Abraham   74f
Linke, Joseph   180
Liszt, Franz   3, 23, 42, 44, 56,
    78, 89
Lockspeiser, Edward   89 n.46
Lodes, Birgit   151 n. 18, 158

London   11, 18, 42, 91, 171 n.3
Loos, Helmut   82 n.32
Lühning, Helge   27 n.26, 29
    n.31

MacArdle, Donald   16, 21
    n.12
Mahling, Christoph-
    Helmut   150 n.15
Mandycewski, Eusebius   47
    n.64, 48, 49 n.68
Marek, George   117, 118 n.2
Marston, Nicholas   77 n.23,
    134
Marx, Adolph Bernhard   16,
    17, 18, 21, 38 n.45, 41f, 43
    n.56, 44, 76, 81, 113 n.22
Massenkeil, Günther   113
    n.22
Massin, Jean and
    Brigitte   140
Meegeren, Han von   30
Mendelssohn, Felix   23, 40,
    50, 91, 92
Metronome markings   26f,
    47, 112
Metternich, Klemens
    von   108
Metzler, Patricia   132 n.25
Meyer, Ernst Hermann   114
Millington, Barry   52 n.73,
    53 n
Morris, Edmund   137f
Moscheles, Ignaz   7 n.9, 18,
    29, 34, 42, 91
Moser, Hans Joachim   50
    n.72, 125
Motley, John Lothrop   39

Mozart, Wolfgang
    Amadeus   2, 8, 35, 38,
    43, 44, 66, 83, 89, 95, 106,
    113 n.25, 121, 126, 127, 133,
    148, 149, 150, 153, 154, 177f
Murry, John Middleton   96

Nazi period   78, 83, 103-110
Neate, Charles   90
Neefe, Christian Gottlob   3,
    147f, 151
Nestjew, Israel   114
Niemetschek, Franz   177
Nohl, Ludwig   13, 17, 18, 41f,
    44ff, 56, 62, 68, 76, 81, 93
Nottebohm, Gustav   17, 18,
    20, 35, 36, 38, 47ff, 51, 56,
    63, 78, 81, 84, 93, 130, 131,
    181

Oulibicheff, Alexander   43,
    56

Pais, Abraham   170, 174f
Paris   11, 16, 17, 20, 42, 53,
    54, 160 n. 40, 178
Pauly, Reinhard   7 n. 9
Penman, Ava Bry   23 n.15,
    175 n.9
Pidcock, George Douglas
    Henzell   83 n. 34
Philosophies
    Eastern   123
    Enlightenment ideals   108,
    109
    Emerson, Ralph Waldo   32
    Hegel, Georg
        Friedrich   133

Hölderlin, Friedrich 133
Kant, Immanuel 32, 65, 108, 122, 133, 176
Indian 123
Marx, Karl 119. 120
Rosicrucian 123
Schelling, Friedrich 133
Schopenhauer, Arthur 53
Transcendentalist movement 32, 33 n.34
Platen, Emil 112, 113
Potter, Cipriani 90
Potter, Pamela 104 n.3, 107 n.10
Prescott, William 39
Prod'homme, Jacques 89
Puccini, Giacomo 66

Ranke, Leopold von 39
Ravel, Maurice 66, 89
Reger, Max 83
Reisinger, Elisabeth 151 n.18, 153
Reynolds, Christopher 52 n.74
Riemann, Hugo 69, 70, 71, 72, 81, 105
Ries, Ferdinand 3, 7, 9, 10, 11, 12 n.16, 15, 17, 20, 27, 34, 53, 54, 58, 76, 87, 90, 115
Ries, Franz 11
Rieter-Biedermann Verlag 50
Riezler, Walter 80, 83ff, 88 n.37
Rig-Veda 123
Rilke, Rainer Maria 178

Ripley, George 33
Robeson, Paul 119
Robbins Landon, Howard Chandler 118
Robinson, J. Bradford 24 n.16
Rochlitz, Friedrich 9
Rolland, Romain 69, 85, 87f, 100, 140
Ronge, Julia 20 n.10, 37, 47 n.65, 158 n.33
Rosen, Charles 83
Rosenfeld, Oskar 105 n.4
Ross, Megan 163 n.44
Russia 7, 23, 42, 43, 108, 113, 114, 118
Ryder, Theodore 104f

Sadie, Stanley 50 n.70, 87 n.43, 114 n.53, 118, 124
Salieri, Antonio 20 n.10, 47
Saloman, Ora Frishberg 33
Schaden, Joseph Wilhelm von 151
Schaffer, Peter 178
Schenk, Erich 110, 111
Schenker, Heinrich 79f, 84f, 94, 112, 130
Schiedermair, Ludwig 69, 82, 106f, 149 n.9
Schiller, Friedrich 22 n.13, 32, 80, 103, 108, 116, 133
Schiller Verein of Trieste 73
Schindler, Anton 5 n.6, 7ff, 10, 13, 15, 16, 17, 18-31, 34, 40f, 43, 46, 49, 50, 51, 53f, 60, 73, 74, 76, 79, 81, 82, 91, 105, 107, 116, 131

Schlesinger, Adolph
  Martin 44
Schlesinger, Maurice 54
Schlosser, Johann Aloys 7f,
  42
Schmidt, Christian
  Martin 24 n.16
Schmidt, Hans 112, 158 n.36
Schmidt-Görg, Joseph 29
  n.30
Schmitt, Carl 82
Schmitz, Arnold 28, 69, 80,
  82
Schoenbaum, Samuel 30
  n.32
Schönberg, Arnold 66, 78,
  89
Schrade, Leo 53, 86
Schreker, Franz 78
Schubert, Franz 83, 92, 121
Schumann, Robert 23, 50,
  52 n.74
Schuppanzigh, Ignaz 180
Schuppanzigh Quartet 5
Scott, Marion 90, 95, 96f
Sebald, Amalie 81
Seigel, Jerrold 67
Seyfried, Ignaz von 20
Shakespeare, William 12,
  30, 86, 145, 177
Shapiro, James 30 n.32, 145
Skelton, Geoffrey 56 n.87
Slochower, Harry 119, 120
  n.5
Slonimsky, Nicolas 24 n.17
Smart, Sir George 90
Solomon, Maynard 5 n.6,
  6 n.7, 13, 45, 71 n.7, 81

n.29, 82, 83 n.33, 115, 116,
  119-23, 131f, 133, 135 n.33,
  136, 137, 142, 147, 148, 150
  n.14, 158, 165 n.46
Spitta, Philipp 38
Spohr, Louis 40, 153
Stadlen, Peter 26, 27 n.26,
  112
Stanley, Glenn 42 n.52, 50
  n.70
Steblin, Rita 8 n. 11
Steinberg, Michael 116
Steinberg, Michael P. 1 n.2,
  99 n.67
Steiner, Anton 4
Stern, Fritz 85f
Stieler, Joseph Karl 23
Stoltzfus, Fred 132 n.25
Strauss, Richard 66
Stravinsky, Igor 66, 89
Strunk, Oliver 124
Sullivan, John William
  Navin 69, 90, 95, 96-9,
  102
Swafford, Jan 137, 138f

Thayer, Alexander
  Wheelock 4, 16, 17, 18,
  24, 26, 31-41, 44, 46, 49f,
  51, 55, 56, 61, 69-75, 78,
  81, 84, 93, 95, 105, 119,
  131, 137, 148 n.5, 155
Thomas-San-Galli,
  Wolfgang 69, 80f
Thomson, George 90
Tolstoy, Leo 88
Tomaschek, Wenzel
  Johann 180

Todd, R. Larry   50 n.71
Tovey, Donald Francis   90,
    93-6, 101, 159f, 170
Treitler, Leo   125 n.14
Trieste   31 n.33, 34, 73
Tyson, Alan   11, 12 n.16, 42
    n.52, 45 n.61, 90, 94 n.58,
    115, 122 n.10, 123, 124,
    126-8, 129, 143, 181

Ullrich, Hermann   5 n.6, 27

Vanguard Records   119
Varèse, Edgard   66
Vermeer, Jan   30
Vienna   1, 3, 5, 8, 9, 10, 11, 12,
    38, 39, 50, 68, 75, 81, 91,
    95, 105, 108, 110-2, 115,
    116, 117f, 122, 127, 136,
    137, 140, 146f, 148-162,
    165, 173, 179
Voltaire   89

Wagner, Cosima   56
Wagner, Richard   17, 18, 23,
    51-6, 78, 81, 82, 89, 128
Wallace, Robin   25 n.30, 179,
    180 n.16

Wasielewski, Wilhelm Joseph
    von   81
Weavers, The   119
Weber, Carl Maria von   3,
    52, 179f
Webster, James   42 n.52, 116
Wegeler, Franz   7, 9-11, 12,
    15, 17, 20, 22, 34, 53f, 59,
    76, 87, 98, 120
Webster, James   42 n.52, 116
Weill, Kurt   78
Weissweiller, Eva   110 n.17
Whittall, Arnold   130 n.24
Willman, Magdalene   79
Wilson, John D.   151, 152, 153
Winkler, Theodor   54
Winter, Robert   29 n.30, 115,
    116, 119, 127, 181
Winterfeld, Carl von   38
Wolff, Christoph   113 n.25
Wolf, Werner   55 n.84

Young, Percy   92 n.53
Young-Bruehl, Elisabeth   23
    n.15, 171, 175ff

Zmeskall von Domanovecz,
    Nikolaus   136